SOMETHING FROM NOTHING

TruthQuest

SOMETHING FROM NOTHING

Understanding What You Believe About Creation and Why

KURT P. WISE
AND
SHEILA A. RICHARDSON

BROADMAN
&HOLMAN
PUBLISHERS

NASHVILLE, TENNESSEE

0-8054-2779-1

Published by Broadman & Holman Publishers,
Nashville, Tennessee

Dewey Decimal Classification: 231.7
Subject Heading: CREATIONISM \ PROVIDENCE AND
GOVERNMENT OF GOD

Unless otherwise stated all Scripture citation is from
the Holman Christian Standard Bible,
© 1999, 2000, 2002, 2003 Holman Bible Publishers.

Credits: Unless noted otherwise, Michael E. Erkel created the
graphics in this book. Other images were provided by Heidi
Howard of Erkel Associates (Crozet, Va.), NASA, VLA-NRAO, U.S.
Department of Energy, Camilla Muluotoga, Steve Austin and the
Institute for Creation Research, and NOAA.

1 2 3 4 5 6 7 8 9 10 08 07 06 05 04

CONTENTS

Part 1

The Why, How, and When of Origins Study

Introduction

What, another book to read? Many of you are currently in high school or college, where much reading is required. The demands of work, church, and social activities probably don't leave a lot of margin for additional reading projects. Perhaps your parents, youth leader, or other well-meaning adult gave this book to you. Yes, some novels are fun for recreational reading, but this book? It isn't an academic book and it isn't a novel—part of it may not even be very easy to read. "Couldn't I wait until it comes out on video?" could well be your natural reaction.

Seriously—this book just may contain some of the most important information you'll ever read (apart from the Scriptures). It is a book about origins, which may answer many of your questions concerning evolution, fossils, dinosaurs, and the Flood. But the goal of this book is not predominantly to answer questions. There are currently many antievolutionary books on the market that critique Darwin and the naturalistic worldview. This book has a deeper purpose.

Part 1, three chapters long, will give you that purpose. It will establish the framework and the reason this book was written. The section deals with the how, why, and when of origins study. Later, part 2 will address some of the fascinating questions concerning origins. You may be tempted to go straight to part 2 instead of dealing with the "whys" and "hows," the more philosophical aspects of the subject. But try to resist. The rewards that will result from your perseverance may surprise you.

Where will he be with the Lord ten years from now?

Photo courtesy of Heidi Howard, Erkel and Associates (Crozet, Va.)

CHAPTER 1

A YOUNG PERSON
GOES TO COLLEGE:
THE *WHY* OF ORIGINS STUDY

MOST of you who are reading this book have arrived at a point in life when you are actively thinking about your future. Is there life after high school? Questions abound: *Do I want to go to college? Where do I want to go to college? What do I want to study? What will I be doing ten years from now?*

Let us pose one more question. Where will you be with the *Lord* ten years from now? Will He have His rightful place in your life? You may at this point answer, "Sure, church activities are very important in my life. I study the Bible. I go to church. I pray. My friends are Christians. Of course God will remain an important part of my life."

News flash! No matter where you go to college—or even *if* you go to college—a major challenge to your faith will confront you in the near future. The pressures to abandon your walk with God will be huge. Will you stand? *How* can you stand?

This book is about origins—the beginning of all things. Strange as it may seem, the study of beginnings—the universe, the earth, life, and mankind—is intimately related to the question of your standing firm in your faith.

As you read this book, we ask you to put yourself into the shoes of a young man we will call Scott (or if you are a woman, substitute

Scott with Susan). His story (actually a true story) is very likely to be your story as you encounter life in our twenty-first-century culture. Many of you will share his experience, regardless of whether you are in college or in the workplace.

First, an introduction. Scott grew up in a middle-class home in the South. He attended church and Sunday school all his life and was taught all the stories: the creation of the world, Adam and Eve, Noah and the ark, and, of course, Jesus and the salvation He offers. Scott attended a Christian high school, graduated with honors, and now wants to become a doctor. As he enters a prestigious Southern university, he is confident in his faith. *Of course* the Bible is true! *Of course* God created the world! Scott knows he belongs to Jesus. He begins his collegiate career full of anticipation and the desire to live a godly and productive life.

On Scott's first day in chemistry class, the professor introduces the course to the group of five hundred students assembled in the auditorium. He begins by saying, "Those of you who are Christians might as well forget your faith right now because you can't be a Christian and an evolutionist, and we know that evolution is a proven fact."

Hmmm, Scott thinks, *This is supposed to be chemistry?* He is somewhat taken aback by the professor's anti-Christian fervor, but he is even more concerned as he looks around the room and sees that a majority of his peers are nodding in agreement with the professor's claim.

In biology class he is quickly told that the entire discipline of biology is built upon evolutionary theory. Life came about by chance and natural law and developed from a single cell up through a chain of organisms culminating with man. The evidence seems well reasoned and is presented in a powerful way in his textbook and lectures. The professor is extremely intelligent, surely more intelligent than his parents and Sunday school teachers. And the other students seem to be buying it . . . more nodding heads.

And so it continues. Scott takes the required humanities class, which declares man the measure of all things. No higher power is necessary. He learns that man invented religion. He hears that abortion is simply a way all animals (of which man is included) can get rid of unwanted offspring. The idea that homosexuality is a lifestyle that should be considered an equal option to heterosexuality is promoted enthusiastically. Christians who oppose or who dare to mention the word *sin* are labeled as intolerant bigots. Physics worships natural laws and declares that these laws "just happened." Truth is loudly proclaimed to be a relative thing—and the only absolute truth allowed is that there is absolutely no absolute truth. The Bible, he is told, is an ancient collection of myths and folklore.

If you were Scott, what would you be thinking right now? Scott is beginning to have some doubts. This "evidence" he is hearing from all sides looks pretty impressive. Besides, all these smart people are ridiculing him and his faith. Even his friends are joining in. Scott feels more and more isolated from his world. He wants to do well in school and even impress his professors. He wants to be liked and accepted by the other students.

What should he do?

What would *you* do?

Is it any wonder that statistics indicate that approximately one out of two professing Christian students entering college walks away (at least temporarily) from his faith?[1] Scott's story is multiplied by thousands each year at colleges and universities throughout the land.

As we continue to accompany Scott on his journey, let's consider three ways he could respond to his situation. We'll look at each option and then discuss the consequences.

Option 1: Join the Crowd

Suppose Scott responds according to the previously stated statistics and buys what the professors and the entire college scene are teaching. He agrees that the Christian faith is unsophisticated, naïve, and intolerant. He decides that his earlier Christian beliefs were for children who didn't really *know*. So Scott joins the secular crowd. He stops going to church. His morals slip, and his behavior becomes the same as a majority of the students. He is able to achieve good grades because when he is tested, he parrots back exactly what he has been told.

What are the consequences for Scott in accepting option 1? Well, we won't say that he has lost his salvation because if he is really saved, God will not let him go; He will lead him back to the truth at some point in his life. But Scott has lost, at least for a season, the joy of life in Christ and the comfort and guidance of the Holy Spirit (whom he has quenched with his sin and disobedience). He has failed to grow in Christlikeness. He has lost the fellowship he could be having with other believers. Even though the Christian students are a minority and are sometimes ridiculed by other students, they are capable of forming deep relationships that unsaved students can never attain. "You will know they are Christians by their love," the popular song (and Bible teaching) goes—and that truth is lost to Scott by choosing option 1. Other consequences of Scott's poor choice involve the wages of sin: he may suffer the results of drug abuse, sexual sin, alcoholism, and other destructive behaviors. Yes, there *is* forgiveness through Christ, but there are also consequences for sin. In addition, he is not serving God or honoring Him. And finally, he is living and believing a lie. He has denied the truth beginning with God's creation and continuing with His Word, and he will incur God's anger and chastisement.

Option 2: Fight, Fight, Fight

There is a second option. Scott gets mad. He knows there are answers. He looks for those answers and becomes a zealous defender of the Christian faith. He goes after evidence that proves that the Bible is true and that God created the world. He spends much of his time challenging his professors in class and engaging his fellow students in lively debate. He has all the answers to how dinosaurs fit into the biblical picture and where Cain got his wife and how radiometric dating can be refuted and how light travels through space. He attacks the "Big Bang" and other various claims of evolutionary theory. He flatly denies all claims of Darwin, and he begins to ridicule evolution and evolutionists. After all, they are ridiculing him for his beliefs, aren't they? Isn't it fair to fight back? He plans to wear down the opposition with his daunting defense of biblical truth. He searches. He stands firm. If God is Who He says He is, then the world we see is *God's* world, and the evidence from God's world will not contradict the evidence from His Word.

What do you think of this option? Granted, when one has no faith or one's faith is threatened, searching out answers to nagging questions can be helpful in removing the obstacles that get in the way of believing God is Who He says He is. Checking out the evidence can be the first step for some in the walk to saving faith. If a person is an unbeliever, he can be drawn by the Holy Spirit to search for God through looking at the things made. Evidences will not in themselves give faith that is necessary for salvation; however, evidences can remove the stumbling blocks that are preventing the person from accepting the things unseen that are required to accept the truth of the gospel. That is why the study of origins can be a powerful evangelistic tool.

But there will be some problems with this view for Scott if chasing after evidence is as far as he goes. Because Scott is a believer, his approach to origins should be much broader than for the unbeliever. He should have a different reason for pursuing the study. We'll list three problems with the "prove it by evidence" option.

1. Does Scott really think the Bible *needs* defending? Does the existence of God *need* proving? Even when its truth is denied by men, it remains true. God manages just fine without us feeling we are needed to *defend* Him.

2. In Hebrews 11:6, we are told that we must come to God by faith. If Scott reasons his way to God with proof, then where does faith come in? How can he please God? Scott (and our) commitment to God should not be dependent upon evidence that

> ### HEBREWS 11:6
> *Now without faith it is impossible to please God, for the one who draws near to Him must believe that He exists and rewards those who seek Him.*

God exists and Creation is true; this causes the evidence to hold a higher authority than God Himself. Scott should look at evidence, but not for the purpose of finding proof that God exists or that God is the Creator. These issues should already be accepted by *faith*.

3. Finally, in depending upon reasonable arguments and physical evidence from the world to defend God and His Creation of the world, Scott has set himself up for a fall. Since fallible men came up with these arguments, many of them will ultimately have been falsified. There goes Scott's faith, down the tubes with the failed argument. The argument is falsified and Scott is devastated. His faith will then rest on the ideas of men rather than the absolute truth of God. Every time another newspaper article appears presenting some exciting new fossil find for evolution, Scott will panic in fear that he has been wrong all along and that indeed evolution will be proven true. By choosing the "prove it by evidence" option, man's thinking, not God's, will rule and ultimately shake Scott's faith. If his faith depends upon human observations and interpretations, then he really doesn't have faith—just human observations and interpretations.

So, while Scott is faring better spiritually with option 2, he still isn't doing very well, is he? Is there another way? Should he forget looking for evidence and just grit his teeth and say, "The Bible tells me so" over and over again a hundred times a day while ignoring the evidence and reasoning presented in his college courses? Does he need to put his head in the sand like the proverbial ostrich and refuse to think through issues? Of course not. There *is* a need to look at evidence, to study the origins issues, and to responsibly study the physical world God created. There is a need to resolve doubts when the doubts are consuming. Much of the remainder of this book will present facts, reasons, and evidences related to origins. There is a profound need to study origins—but not to prove that God exists or that the Bible is true. The study of origins is broader and much more important than merely finding answers or trying to prove absolute truth that doesn't need proving. The study of origins is closely related to each person's understanding of himself and his Creator. In fact, one's thinking about one's *origin* will most likely be the major influence in the understanding of one's *destiny*.

Option 3: Think of the Artist and His Masterpiece

This final option involves a three-step process:

Step 1: Remember the Truth You Already Know

Scott has begun to have some doubts. The first thing he needs to do is remember the teachings he knows from his youth. He needs to pray and ask the Spirit to remind him of some very basic truths.

- The study of origins is the study of *beginnings*. Scott knows that even before the beginning, there was God. God is all that was before the beginning. The where, when, how, why, and who of the beginning of everything that began is God. God's truth is what must be used to properly interpret all the data of the universe. *God* must be the central focus of all origins study.

- He also remembers that God requires faith—complete trust and dependence on Him. Logic, reason, and knowledge play important roles, but faith must carry the day. If we could reason our way to God with proofs and evidence, then faith would not be necessary. Scripture teaches that we walk by faith, not by sight (2 Corinthians 5:7).

- Scott recalls that as a youngster he assumed by faith that God's Word is true. He doesn't need to seek evidence for the existence of God or the truth of Scripture. Rather, he *starts* with that assumption.

Step 2: Look at the Creation and See What You Learn

Romans 1:18–20 is printed in a box on the next page. Let's consider this passage for a few moments. It begins in verse 18 by telling us that God is angry because there are sinful, wicked people who push away truth. They know this truth, but they refuse to accept it

ROMANS 1:18-20

[18]*For God's wrath is revealed from heaven against all godlessness and unrighteousness of people who by their unrighteousness suppress the truth,* [19]*since what can be known about God is evident among them, because God has shown it to them.* [20]*From the creation of the world His invisible attributes, that is, His eternal power and divine nature, have been clearly seen, being understood through what He has made. As a result, people are without excuse.*

even though there is clear evidence. We all know people like that.

Can you see from verse 20 what that evidence is and what it shows? The verse tells us that since the world began, people have been able to clearly see the evidence of God's Creation. It isn't hidden; it is very clear.

But the passage also tells us what we learn about *God* from this evidence. Do you see it in verse 20? We are told that just from seeing the creation we are able to see some of God's invisible attributes: His eternal power and divine nature—invisible things (the character of God)—all from the creation.

Can you tell then why Scott (and any believer) needs to study the creation? If your answer is to learn more about God—His eternal power and divine nature—you are correct.

Step 3: Learn about the Artist from His Masterpiece; Learn about the Masterpiece from the Artist

Have you ever been attracted to a particular work of art? Let's say you see a painting by Picasso, and you are fascinated. What a weird painting! You study the colors, the impressions given. You ponder its meaning. You are then drawn to learn more about the artist himself. Who was this person? What in his character and life experience led him to create the strange-looking art he created? As you learn more of the artist, you then come to appreciate (or at least understand) even more the works of art he created, which in turn teaches you more about the artist. And so it continues.

The same is true of music. Assume you love classical music and have been playing Tchaikovsky's Fifth Symphony. The symphony moves you to strong emotion by its powerful themes and chords.

That leads you to wonder about the man who created this masterpiece. What in his character led him to compose music of this nature? What happened in his life to influence his music? Again, as you learn more about the creator of the music, you then appreciate more of his works, which leads you to learn even more about the person who composed them.

Consider films. If you love the Tolkien movie *Lord of the Rings,* that may lead you to discover more about J. R. R. Tolkien. What was his worldview? Was he a Christian? What is he revealing through the fantasy of orcs and hobbits, evil and good? After seeing the movie, you want to read the books, to go into more detail. The more you study Tolkien and his writings, the more you understand his creation and appreciate the mind behind the created works.

The greatest artist of all is God. His masterpiece is His creation in all its depth and breadth. As you see the created order, you look naturally to the Creator. His Word tells us that this creation reveals many of the characteristics of the Creator—His power and divine attributes. The more you learn about this Creator, the more you see and appreciate and want to study His creation.

> **PSALM 111:2**
>
> *The LORD's works are great, studied by all who delight in them.*

Not only is the physical universe the direct result of God's nature, but it is created in such a way that even a basic understanding of it can lead to an understanding of God. The *why* of origins study for Scott and all believers is to enlarge his understanding of God. As God's works are studied, He becomes larger and larger, and the believer begins to more fully understand and know Him.

The believer should not be seeking evidence of God or of God as Creator. This sets the evidence as a higher authority than God. Rather, he should be seeking a greater understanding of both the creation and the Creator based on the starting point that God is the Creator and that the creation is created.

When Scott begins to study origins because he delights in the works of the Lord and seeks to better know Him, he will benefit in many ways. Some of the benefits include:

- A greater awe of God. He is the One Who "made the heavens and earth by [His] great power and with [His] outstretched arm. Nothing is too difficult for [Him]!" (Jeremiah 32:17).
- A greater understanding of our accountability to the One who is all-powerful. God made us. We belong to Him. He tells us what is best for us, directs our paths, and makes the rules. A human artist is in control of the destiny and purpose of his work of art. Even more so, the Heavenly Artist knows and directs those He made in His image.
- Ability to worship Him better. As we look at the night sky, listen to a symphony, or study the beauty and complexity of any created thing, we are given pictures, shadows of eternal things. God created things that are beautiful and awesome in order to help us see spiritual truths that we otherwise can't easily comprehend.
- Ability to glorify Him in all things. Our lives will have purpose and direction and will be used for the Master's purposes.
- A greater understanding of the created order.
- A better understanding of self in relationship to God and to others.
- An increased understanding of the mind and heart of God and in turn growth in learning to think God's thoughts and have the mind of Christ.
- A better understanding of theology and how all human thought can be brought under the umbrella of biblical understanding.
- A greater ethic. We will be better able to choose the excellent path as we make decisions concerning right and wrong in our life's walk.

Ten years from now, what will *really* matter in your life will be your relationship with your God. Fancy jobs, material possessions, even personal relationships pale in comparison.

What's Next?

The question of why origins should be studied has been addressed. Logically, the next step to follow is to ask *how?* Where does one begin this study? How does one approach the study, and where does he go to get the information? This will be the subject of the next chapter.

Consider the Concept

The person who seriously studies and understands origins is more likely to know and honor his Creator.

Questions to Ponder

- Think for a moment about the statement that approximately one out of every two people walks away from the Christian faith in the years immediately following high school. Why do you believe this happens?
- In this chapter, the challenges to Scott's faith could be responded to in three ways. Review those three options. How would each choice affect his life in the years following?
- What role does faith play in the way one should approach the study of origins?
- If you were "best friends" with J. R. R. Tolkien, how would knowing him personally make a difference in your understanding and appreciating his masterpiece *The Lord of the Rings*? Conversely, what would reading the LOTR books or watching the film teach you about the mind and heart of Tolkien? Apply those thoughts to the Creator of the universe and the value of studying origins.
- If you could take only *one* thought/principle to remember from this chapter, what would it be?

A Verse to Remember

The LORD's works are great,
studied by all who delight in them. . . .

He has caused His wonderful works to be remembered.
The LORD is gracious and compassionate.

Psalm 111:2, 4

CHAPTER 2
GOD'S WORD AND GOD'S WORLD: THE *HOW* OF ORIGINS STUDY

OUR student, Scott (and hopefully also you, the reader), has determined that he is going to study origins because he wants his understanding of God to encompass all that is known and all that is. He wants to know God. Now, where does he begin?

What's Wrong with This Picture?

The following are some comments one might hear in many of our churches today:

- "Science has taught us that the body of man evolved from the body of some apelike creature. So, obviously the part of Genesis that tells us that God formed Adam from the dust of the ground is in error. We need then to understand that Genesis is a creation myth. God used evolution in the creation of Adam."

- "Genesis says that light was created on the first day of Creation Week, but the sun wasn't created until the fourth day. Obviously that can't be true. Therefore we must consider that the days of Creation Week aren't really chronological days, and we need to understand Genesis, chapter 1, as merely a way of speaking that intends to say simply that 'God created.' Time isn't an issue here."

- "Radiometric dating techniques have proved that the universe and earth are billions of years old. Therefore, the dates given in the Bible must be wrong. The Bible was written by primitive people who didn't know modern science."

What's wrong with this approach? In all cases mentioned above, the interpretations of modern science have been given authority over the Word of God. Even pastors who should know better knuckle under to the supposed authority of "science." The result is that the Bible is bent and twisted to somehow accommodate man's interpretation of God's world.

Obviously, Scott should not approach the study of origins this way.

First Priority: It All Begins with God's *Word*

It is important that Scott (and you the reader) understand several important points about Scripture and the study of origins.

- First, basic to all else, we start with what God is like. We note, for example, that God is a *communicator*. He does it better than anyone else. He has wanted to teach us, relate to us, and love us since the very beginning of time (and before). This is part of His character. His desire to communicate with us has been so strong that He sent His Word in different ways: directly to prophets and other people at times, in His written Word, and through His Son incarnate.

  Because communication involves receiving as well as sending, God expects us to respond to what He has communicated.

  We then would expect that the Master Communicator would write His Word in a straightforward (natural) fashion, in a way that is clear and understandable. If He didn't do that, He wouldn't be communicating!

  He also would communicate truth in such a way that it would be true throughout time.

- Second, as a consequence of the first point, Scripture is *true*. It holds authority over every other form of knowledge. Scripture proclaims itself to be inspired (the literal word means "God-breathed"). If God, Who is truth itself, "breathes" the words that are written, then those words are totally true. When we study Creation, we must understand that God was the only eyewitness, and eyewitness evidence is the best.

This means that straightforward statements of Scripture should be considered truth whether they refer to "spiritual" truth, "scientific" truth, or "historical" truth. The authority of the Word is *not* limited to morality and lifestyle or to spiritual matters alone.

> **2 TIMOTHY 3:16**
>
> *All Scripture is inspired by God and is profitable for teaching, for rebuking, for correcting, for training in righteousness.*

The hermeneutic (the way one interprets the Bible) that best fits our understanding of God is called the "historico-grammatical" interpretation of Scripture. This interpretation is the most straightforward and is most in line with the nature of God as Communicator. This is the method of interpretation followed in this book.

- Finally, we need to make an interesting observation about Scripture. While it is true that most of the Bible is clear, there are some things that are hard to understand. While the Bible tells us what we *need* to know, it doesn't always tell us everything we *want* to know. There seems to be some ambiguity in God's Word. Some passages seem to have several possible meanings, while others seem veiled or mysterious. We might also observe that the same thing is true in the physical world—in things related to origins. While the creation proclaims truth to us, all things aren't completely understandable. There is some ambiguity.

Can you think of a reason why God doesn't give us *all* the answers in the Scripture or in the creation? We discussed this in the last chapter. God did not give us all the answers because if He did, there would be no need for *faith*. And without faith it is impossible to come to God.

Physical Evidence: Next Look to God's *World*

There are also some important principles about the study of God's *world* that Scott (and you, the reader) should recognize.

- *Science* is the process of studying the physical world. Since God created the physical world so all people everywhere through all time could come to know Him through it, then the foundation for all of science is found in the truth of Scripture and the nature of Who God is.

- *The way it used to be.* Several centuries ago, theology (the study of God) was considered to be the "queen of the sciences" because all disciplines of human thought believed God the Creator central to their development. Modern science was born into this way of thinking. The majority of the original great scientists—Johann Kepler, the founder of physical astronomy; Francis Bacon, who established the "scientific method"; Blaise Pascal, a great philosopher and mathematician; Robert Boyle, founder of modern chemistry; Isaac Newton, who identified laws of motion and gravitation; Carolus Linnaeus, the father of biological taxonomy[1]—were men of God.

  Furthermore, all of the *presuppositions* of science as it developed were based upon a biblical view of God. Presuppositions are assumptions or values that must be accepted as true in order to study the physical world and justify the study of it. One of the presuppositions of modern science includes the fact that the physical world really exists. (You'd be amazed at how many people say that it does *not*.) Another is that the physical world has a reliable structure and order (because God is an unchanging God). Also, the physical world is understandable by humans (because God desires to reveal Himself to man through the creation). Another presupposition is that patterns should remain constant through time and space (because God wants to be seen by all people). There are many more, and all are dependent upon a theistic view of the world.

• *The way it is now.* Something referred to as the "Great Divorce" happened during the last two hundred years. Learned men began to reject God; consequently, the various disciplines of science were cut loose from the glue that held them together. Scientists, for example, were often agnostic or atheistic, and their human reasoning and their anti-God beliefs influenced how they interpreted the physical world. Indeed, if such nonbiblical worldviews continue to dominate the academic world, science as we know it is likely to become extinct (except for the applied sciences, such as medicine and engineering). For example, today's postmodern worldview incorporates some of the presuppositions of pantheism (also called transcendentalism). The pantheistic worldview makes the assertion that the physical world is not consistent enough to be studied or interpreted the same way by all people. Since the transcendent worldview denies the physical, science would be a study of nothing at all!

• *The way it should be.* A reverse of current trends needs to happen. We call it the "Great Synthesis." Believers should seek to restore God to the center of human thought. Scripture should be the basis upon which all philosophies are grounded. Biology, chemistry, physics, psychology, history, geology—all disciplines should have the truths of God's Word as their foundation.

A Case Study: Putting Principles into Practice

As you read the principles above, did they make sense to you? What difference do these things make in your life? How should Scott proceed in his study of origins in light of the information given above?

Let's make it practical.

Scott enters his biology classroom where a study of the cell is taking place. Students are called upon to make observations of the data: the way the cell looks and acts, the parts that can be observed. Once the observations of the data are made, interpretations—explanations of the meaning of the data—follow. It is at this point that Scott must be discerning because *the explanations of the data will reflect the presuppositions held by the interpreter.* If the professor or the textbook's view of God is that He doesn't exist, then their interpretation will deny God's design in the complexity of the cell, arriving instead at some naturalistic explanation. If the person who is interpreting the data is a Christian, he will see the beauty, complexity, and creative design of God that cries out to be recognized in every living thing. He will see the Artist by examining the masterpiece of design that is the cell. This is why the ability to discern the presuppositions behind an interpretation is an invaluable tool for any student.

So, let's assume the teacher gives a naturalistic, evolutionary explanation for the data observed about the cell. Because Scott believes the Bible is foundational to all truth in the universe, he will know to reject *any* explanation of the data that contradicts the truth of Scripture. (In the interest of surviving academically, he may have to parrot back the teacher's interpretation on the test, but in his heart he will reject it.)

He then will be challenged to return to the data and look for an interpretation consistent with God's revelation in Scripture. Whatever Scott comes up with must also be tested, since there may be multiple interpretations possible. The explanation he chooses may prove eventually to be false, but he won't be discouraged because he knows Scripture contains absolute truth. He simply goes back and finds another interpretation, still keeping his theories consistent with Scripture.

Furthermore, he knows that God does not give all answers, either in Scripture or in the physical world, because there is a role to be played by faith. So he stays strong in the faith God abundantly supplies.

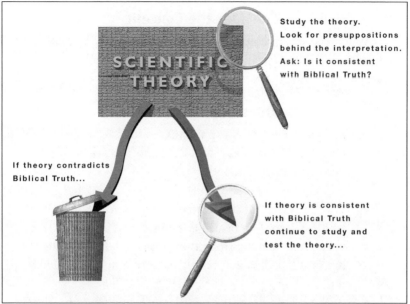

Study the theory.
Look for presuppositions
behind the interpretation.
Ask: Is it consistent
with Biblical Truth?

If theory contradicts
Biblical Truth...

If theory is consistent
with Biblical Truth
continue to study and
test the theory...

*How does one evaluate the truth claims of the many theories to which he is
exposed? The above diagram outlines a useful procedure.*

Graphic courtesy of Erkel and Associates (Crozet, Va.)

Scott (and you) can hold his head high and be excited about
what he is learning about the Artist (the Creator) through His masterpiece (the physical world). What's more, he remains available to
be used by God as he continues to grow as a human being in a way
that will honor the Creator.

What's Next?

Now that you recognize the basic points about God's Word and
world, the role of faith, and the purpose of origins study, let's study
origins! We set the stage in the next chapter by looking at one of the
stumbling blocks to many believers: the age of things. First we'll
look at the Bible (because it is the authority that tells us about the
Artist) to see what it indicates about time. Then we'll look at God's
world (the masterpiece) and the physical evidence we have, as well
as the challenges we still face (the things we still don't understand,
where further study and faith are required).

Consider the Concept

When the interpretation of a theory about the natural world contradicts a clear teaching of Scripture, that theory should be trashed.

Questions to Ponder

- In this chapter, God is presented as the "Great Communicator." How does He communicate, and what difference does it make to you?
- Is God ever ambiguous in His Word? Explain.
- What was the "Great Divorce" as explained in this chapter? How can it be healed (see the "Great Synthesis")?
- When you, like the student in this chapter, encounter teachings in class that "trash" Scripture, what should you do?
- If you could take only one thought/principle from this chapter to use in your daily life, what would it be?

A Verse to Remember

Open my eyes so that I may see
wonderful things in Your law.

Psalm 119:18

CHAPTER 3
HOW OLD IS *OLD?*
THE *WHEN* OF ORIGINS STUDY

BECAUSE a serious study of origins normally begins with Genesis 1—the narrative of the six days of Creation—our inquiring student, Scott, is immediately faced with the most serious challenge to a biblical study of Creation that he will encounter. Six *days?* Is the Bible really trying to tell us that all the complexity of the universe and earth and life came about in six *days*? Isn't that rather naïve? Doesn't *everyone* know that the ages of the earth and the universe are measured in billions of years? "Science" has been telling us that for almost two centuries.

It is amazing how emotionally charged the issue of the age of things is, even among Christians who believe in God as Creator. The general acceptance of great antiquity permeates our lives, from Saturday morning cartoon shows to newspapers, magazines, museums, national parks, roadside signs, and of course, academia. *Especially* academia. Educated Christians are afraid to even entertain the idea that the cosmos is relatively young; to do so somehow threatens their sense of intellectual pride. They fear they will then be lumped with the "fundamentalists" who supposedly even believe the earth is flat. So, Scott needs to be prepared for some emotional outbursts and ridicule as he pursues this issue.

First Priority:
Begin with the Word—Begin with the Artist

Because Scott has chosen to consider God's Word about the world to be authoritative over the theories of men, he turns first to Scripture. Remember, the ultimate goal of origins study is to know the God Who created all things. We learn more of Him as we study the creation, and, in turn, we learn truth about the creation as we come to know more of Him. So, what do we already know about God's character and ways that will help with the age issue?

The Artist Is a Communicator

God doesn't tell us all we might like to know in Scripture. There are mysteries that we are not to understand at this time; there is figurative language and prophecy that is often fuzzy. (Remember, if He told us everything, there would be no need for faith, and without faith we can't please Him.) However, *God communicates effectively what He wants us to know.* He repeats Himself. He "shouts" truth. Although He speaks of Creation in poetic terms in numerous places in Scripture, He presents the story of His Creation in Genesis in a straightforward, historical narrative prose. Most Hebrew scholars agree that Genesis 1 and 2 is Hebrew prose. Though it includes repetition and form and is beautiful enough to be poetic, it is not Hebrew poetry—it is prose.[1]

The Artist's Incredible Attributes

Because God is omnipotent (all-powerful), we can conclude that He is able to create any way He desires—at the twinkling of an eye or in billions of years. He doesn't need billions of years; neither did He need six days. God's eternal nature suggests that the amount of time involved would mean nothing to Him ("with the Lord one day is like 1,000 years, and 1,000 years like one day" [2 Peter 3:8]). A billion years would mean nothing more to Him than six days or no time at all. Although His eternal nature might be better shown in eons of time of Creation, the Bible illustrates His power through the instantaneity of Creation ("For He spoke, and it came into being; He commanded, and it came into existence" [Psalm 33:9]). Also, the wisdom of God would suggest efficiency. It would seem that the less time He took, the more His wisdom would be demonstrated.

The Artist Is King of the Universe

Another very interesting clue follows from Who God is. God is the great King of the universe. Even earthly kings are sovereign over their domains, and they expect instantaneous response to their commands. When they give a command, the subject is expected to obey immediately. Only a disobedient subject would fail to do so. How much more would you expect an unfallen, perfect creation to obey a command from its Creator?

Genesis 1 is filled with verbs that in the Hebrew language are called *jussives of command.* Repeatedly, God says, "Let there be. . . ." Creation was a series of commands from the King of kings. That there was instantaneous obedience is suggested by the comment "and it was so!" Elsewhere in Scripture similar statements suggest immediate response to God's commands. Psalm 33:6 says, "The heavens were made by the word of the LORD, and all the stars, by the breath of His mouth."

God's sovereignty and God's wisdom suggest that instantaneous Creation is most consistent with His nature. But the Creation account claims it took a week. Why?

Creation in a Week

At one point in His ministry, Jesus' disciples were condemned for collecting food ("working?") on the Sabbath. The Creator of the Sabbath responded to the charges by saying that "the Sabbath was made for man, and not man for the Sabbath" (Mark 2:27). What did He mean by this? In Exodus 20:11 God burned into rock His rationale for the Sabbath. We can infer from these two passages that God took as long as a week to create as an *example* to man. This is similar to other instances of dealing with man—His being born as a man, living as a man, being baptized, becoming man's sin out of His love for us, and so on. God chose to do many things that would otherwise be understood as contrary to His nature. Because God created man in such a way as to *require* regular rest, His creating over a period as long as a human work week and then *resting*—even when He did not have to—was done as an example to man.

EXODUS 20:11

For the LORD made the heavens and the earth, the sea, and everything in them in six days; then He rested on the seventh day. Therefore the LORD blessed the Sabbath day and declared it holy.

We can understand, then, from God's nature why He would take as long as a week to create. There is, however, *no* explanation for why He would take any longer than that.

The Much Debated "Day"

But what if the "day" of Genesis 1 is just a picture of the human day, that it was actually longer? Since it makes no difference to God, maybe a million or a billion years of real time simply *represented* a human work week. Space does not allow a complete treatment of this contentious proposition, but consider the following:

- God's wisdom would favor a time period closer to instantaneous (discussed under "The Artist's Incredible Attributes" above).

GENESIS 1:5

God called the light "day," and He called the darkness "night." Evening came, and then morning: the first day.

- The first mention of the word *day* (*yom* in Hebrew) in the entire Bible is found in Genesis 1:5. Is it likely that the very first time a word is mentioned, it would be in a figurative and not a literal sense? That wouldn't make any sense at all! Furthermore, light is the basis of all meanings of day (light, daylight, the day/night cycle), leaving no basis for a meaning of a long period of time.

- God specifies the division between day and night, light and darkness. It is a real stretch to think He is talking about millions or billions of years of light followed by approximately the same period of darkness. Also, millions of years between the creation of plants on Day 3 and pollinating insects on Day 5 would not seem possible. In the straightforward sense, *day* can only mean a day similar to our twenty-four-hour days as they are divided into light and darkness.

- In Genesis 1 we read of many things: *land, trees,* the *expanse, living things,* etc. No one suggests any of these terms should be interpreted symbolically. Why then should *day* be singled out?

- God goes even farther in using the expression *first day, second day, third day,* and so on. When Scripture associates a number with the word *day,* it means a day in the usual sense of the word. (Check it out in your concordance or a Bible computer program.)

- The *jussives of command* and the phrase *it was so* suggest instantaneous obedience (see discussion under "The Artist Is King of the Universe").

- The same Hebrew word in Exodus 20:11 (*yamin*) used to describe the days of the human work week is used in Genesis to describe the days of Creation.

- Whenever the phrase *evening and morning* is used in Scripture, it refers to a twenty-four-hour day.

All of these points seem to clearly indicate that God—the Communicating Artist—created all things in instantaneous bursts over the course of six literal twenty-four-hour days of human time.

Chronologies and Genealogies

If then we conclude that the week of Creation was indeed what the Bible says—a week as we know it—there remains the years *after* that first week. Can we tell from Scripture itself how many years have elapsed since Creation Week? Do the books of the Bible come with dates attached? Is there any other span of history where we can put the millions of years attributed by the conventional model of the earth's age?

It is interesting that archaeology and history give us pretty good evidence for the number of years between Abraham and Christ and between Christ and modern times, and those dates correspond with dates calculated from the Bible. The only periods where archaeological and historical records are seriously lacking outside of Scripture are the years between Creation and the Flood and the years between the Flood and Abraham.

To cover this lack, our communicating God gave us two genealogies (lists of family descent) in Scripture that were distinctly different from the many other genealogies in His Word. These two lists are found in Genesis 5 and 11. In them the Bible specifically provides the ages of fathers at the births of their sons—exactly the kind of information needed to develop a chronology. These lists also give us each individual's time of death and how long they lived. From these biblical records we learn that there were 1,656 years between Creation and the Flood and 342 years between the Flood and the birth of Abraham. These genealogies are all we need to calculate this figure, and they are the only genealogies written in a form that allows them to be used as chronologies. The information they provide firmly establishes the creation as approximately 6,000 years old.

Physical Evidence: What Does It Tell Us about Age?

Our inquiring student, Scott, must conclude that biblical evidences seem to indicate that the Bible leaves no place for the billions-of-years theory for the history of the universe—or even millions or tens of thousands of years. He has already affirmed that Scripture has the authority and is to be the reference point for all scientific study. In fact, Scripture gives an eyewitness to these things—the *only* eyewitness. And Scott knows that the Creator is trustworthy; He will not deceive.

But it's so tough! Things *look* old. How can someone look at mountains and canyons and not think *old?* And what about the "absolute ages" in radiometric dating methods? Then there is carbon dating . . . and those dinosaurs that roamed the earth before man ever appeared . . . and those claims of apelike human ancestors . . . and the huge universe . . . and the travel of light through space. The questions go on and on. What is Scott to do?

First of all, he needs to remember what we all must do when the physical seems to contradict the biblical, eyewitness report. We are to reject the interpretation that contradicts Scripture and then go back and look at the evidence and see what interpretation can be found that *is* in accord with biblical truth. In fact, that is exactly what creation research scientists are doing today—they are in the process of reinterpreting the data in ways that are consistent with Scripture.

The earth's age is truly a complex topic, and this chapter barely skims the surface. There are challenges to creation research, and complete, definitive answers to all the questions don't yet exist. More research is needed. God has provided interesting evidence for the young-age and against the old-age hypothesis, but questions remain. (Does that surprise you? Once again, faith is needed because God requires faith.)

Some Interesting Considerations

Many of Scott's questions will be addressed in later chapters that deal with geology, anthropology, and living things. As this chapter draws to a conclusion, however, let's look at a few interesting considerations with regard to the age of things.

Appearance of Age

We must conclude that God can and does create things that appear much older than they really are. For example, when Jesus created the wine at the wedding in Cana (John 2:1–10), people naturally assumed that the wine had been made by growing, processing, and fermenting the grapes, then placing the resulting beverage in containers to transport to the wedding feast.

If you had been present to meet Adam after he was created from the dust of the ground, you might have assumed (falsely, of course) that he had grown from an embryo, through childhood, and into young adulthood.

If you had looked at the trees bearing fruit on the third day of Creation, you might have assumed they began with a seed that

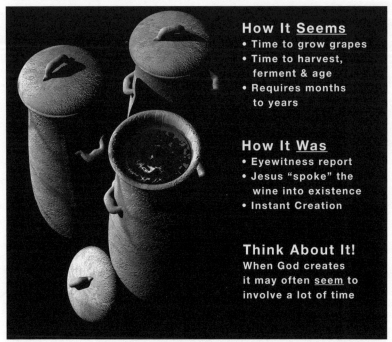

How It <u>Seems</u>
- Time to grow grapes
- Time to harvest, ferment & age
- Requires months to years

How It <u>Was</u>
- Eyewitness report
- Jesus "spoke" the wine into existence
- Instant Creation

Think About It!
When God creates it may often <u>seem</u> to involve a lot of time

The story of Jesus' creation of wine from water (John 2:1–10) gives interesting insight into the appearance of age in created things.

Erkel and Associates (Crozet, Va.)

grew into a seedling and then into a tree that finally produced mature fruit.

If you were with Jesus when He fed the five thousand and you hadn't directly seen Him perform the miracle, you might have assumed that all of the bread and fish that was consumed had some sort of history of growing, catching, and preparing associated with them.

But Scripture teaches us that these events happened *instantaneously* through an act of God.

God provides sufficient ambiguity in the Creation for humans to conclude erroneously a history that never actually occurred—*if they so choose*—because God requires faith of us. But He also provides the truth in the account He gives us, and He provides evidence against the alternative hypotheses.

So when you look at a mountain or a canyon or a fossil or things that are credited to millions of years of evolution, remember the Cana wine, the miracles, the eyewitness reports . . . and question and think in a fresh way about the interpretation you have been given.

Carbon-14 Dating

Carbon dating is used to date things that were once living. An oversimplified explanation follows:

There are different forms of carbon. Carbon-12(^{12}C) is by far the most common form. Carbon-14(^{14}C) is known as radiocarbon, and it is made when cosmic rays knock neutrons out of atomic nuclei in the upper atmosphere.

^{14}C is radioactive, which means it is unstable and decays, eventually changing back into nitrogen.

Carbon—both ^{12}C and ^{14}C—is found in the atmosphere in the form of carbon dioxide and in all organisms in the form of organic molecules. While a plant or animal is alive, it is constantly exchanging carbon with its surroundings, keeping the same $^{12}C/^{14}C$ ratio found in the air.

However, once a plant or animal dies, the ^{14}C atoms that decay are no longer replaced, so while the amount of ^{12}C remains constant, the ^{14}C declines, and the ratio changes. The relative amount of ^{14}C and ^{12}C provides a "clock" to help estimate an age for the once-living organism.

Carbon dating gives results in the thousands, not millions, of years. However, it generally gives dates that still are larger than the six thousand years a young-age creationist would assign to the earth and universe. How can we explain the supposed discrepancy with the Bible's chronology?

The answer that seems to be emerging is fascinating. If the earth has had a stable atmosphere for longer than thirty thousand years, as is generally assumed, then ^{14}C should be in secular equilibrium (that is, the amount of ^{14}C produced in the upper atmosphere should be equal to the amount of ^{14}C breaking down by radioactive decay). In fact, however, the earth's atmosphere is 20 percent short of secular equilibrium. This may be related to what we see in tree-ring studies, where one would expect the dates of tree rings to correspond to the ages one gets by counting rings. Yet tree-ring ages begin diverging from ^{14}C ages before about 1000 B.C.

These facts, combined with biblical dating, suggest that the equilibrium is off because the earth hasn't been around for thirty thousand years. When appropriate corrections are made based on a biblical view of history, carbon dates that result come much closer to biblical dates. Creationist scientists are confident a complete reconciliation will eventually be accomplished.

Radiometric Dating

Radiometric dating methods other than Carbon-14 are used to date igneous (once molten) rocks, and these are the methods that give results in millions or billions of years. These techniques use the relative concentrations of parent and daughter products in radioactive decay series. This book obviously does not have space for a detailed explanation and critique of the dating techniques used today, but many challenges exist to the claim that they truly give "absolute age" as claimed. There are many dating methods, and each method runs into difficulty with at least some data. It is not usually enough to *totally* falsify the method, but enough to question the conclusions.

- For example, in the case of potassium-argon (K-Ar) dating, potassium (the parent) decays over time into argon (the daughter). When molten lava flows over the earth's surface, argon (as a gas) should escape from the lava before it

· ·

Carbon dating can be a useful tool for dating things that were once living. It gives dates in thousands, not millions, of years. When corrected for equilibrium imbalance, carbon dating results come quite close to biblical dates.   Erkel and Associates (Crozet, Va.)

Cosmic Rays bombard the upper atmosphere
producing hyper-accelerated neutrons

These collide with Nitrogen in the atmosphere
producing Carbon-14 (^{14}C)

^{14}C combines with oxygen
to produce carbon dioxide
(CO_2). During photosynthesis
vegetation absorbs the CO_2
containing the ^{14}C

Since animals feed on vegetation
^{14}C is added to their bodies at
the present rate of about
1 in 1,000,000,000,000 atoms

^{14}C Loss by decay

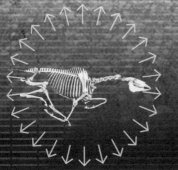

After death this ratio will
slowly decrease ^{14}C continues to
decay and is not replenished by
feeding. The amount of ^{14}C in a
dead animal shows how long it
has been dead - provided one
knows the amount of ^{14}C in
the animal when it died.

cools. Therefore, the K-Ar age of new lava flows should be zero. In actuality, recent lava flows have not lost all their argon. Rather than having an age of zero, they consistently yield ages of hundreds of thousands of years (to millions of years for individual minerals).[2]

- When one takes a single rock and "dates" it using multiple, different dating techniques, it should in theory produce the same age. In actuality, however, multiple methods usually yield multiple ages—that are not even close.[3]

- If radioactive decay (especially uranium and thorium decay) has been occurring for billions of years, there should be a lot more helium in the atmosphere than there actually is.[4]

- The fact that all these methods have problems suggests that something is not quite right with the methods. Although we cannot as yet provide sufficient evidence to prove them wrong, the problems they have do provide sufficient reason to seek a better explanation. And once a clearer understanding and interpretation of the methods is found, radiometric dating will likely reveal ages compatible with the biblical record and will then become a valuable tool for use by creation scientists.

Other Considerations

The following considerations (and there are many more than these listed here) provide interesting challenges to the conventional way of thinking about age:

- If there had been a period in earth history when radiometric decay rates were higher than they are at present (such as when God brought judgment during the Flood), then the radiometric ages we see today would be too old.[5]

- If the speed of light was once faster than is now measured, and/or if the universe had superstrong distortions in the fourth dimension, and/or if the universe has a sufficiently nonuniform distribution of mass-energy, then light might

be able to travel substantially farther than would be otherwise expected in a six-thousand-year-old universe.

- The Creation model suggests lava was produced at much
  higher rates and under much more water during the Flood
  than is believed in non-Flood geology. Less argon gas
  would have been released under these conditions, leaving
  the lavas with K-Ar ages that are too old.

- Precipitation rates and temperatures are thought to have
  been very high immediately after the Flood and to have
  decreased exponentially after that. A number of processes
  used to give the age of things are dependent upon temperature and rainfall.

- High precipitation rates in early post-Flood times may also
  be capable of accumulating the large ice sheets currently
  found in Greenland and Antarctica.[6]

- Earth catastrophes and high precipitation rates during and
  after the Flood would have generated extremely high erosion and sedimentation rates. If estimated using modern
  rates, these anomalies would result in consistently exag-
  gerated ages.

- In the current Creation model, the earth's initial magnetic
  field may have been sixteen to thirty-two times stronger
  than the present field. Such a strong magnetic field would
  have deflected many cosmic rays, resulting in very low,
  pre-Flood ^{14}C production. There may also have been a
  more stratified atmosphere before the Flood, resulting in
  less of the heavy carbon dioxide making its way to the
  earth's surface. There was probably also more carbon dioxide in the early earth atmosphere, with much of it being
  captured in limestone during the Flood. This would have
  diluted any heavy carbon dioxide that did make it to the
  surface. As a result, there may have been little to no ^{14}C
  based carbon dioxide in the pre-Flood atmosphere.
  Without ^{14}C in the air, there may have been no ^{14}C in
  organisms before the Flood. In light of this, ^{14}C ages will

be increasingly too old as the true age gets closer to the Flood.[7]

So What? Does Age Really Matter?

Many Christians would say age doesn't matter. We hear the statement "We don't need to be concerned about the age of rocks; rather we need to consider the Rock of Ages." While that sounds pious, the person who says that hasn't really given the subject much thought. Age *does* matter.

Following are some of the ways it matters:

If the conventional, old-age model of origins is true—

> *Then* Genesis got it wrong about the sequence of created things. Earth was *not* created before the sun (Genesis 1:9, 14) as stated.

If the conventional, old-age model of origins is true—

> *Then* Genesis got it wrong because it says flying creatures were created before land animals and fruit trees before sea creatures (Genesis 1:11, 20, 24).

If the conventional, old-age model of origins is true—

> *Then* Genesis got it wrong when it claims men and animals were vegetarians in Genesis 1:29–30 (since the fossil record interpreted as a record of long ages shows carnivory [animals eating animals] long before man came to be).

If the conventional, old-age model of origins is true—

> *Then* God got it wrong when He said all the creation was "very good," in Genesis 1:31 (because in the long ages way of looking at things, by the time man was created there had been millions of years of disease, suffering, and catastrophe in the world).

If the conventional, old-age model of origins is true—

> *Then* Genesis 2:7 got it wrong when man was formed from dust rather than from some apelike creature. It would be equally wrong in claiming that Eve came from the side of Adam.

If the conventional, old-age model of origins is true—
> *Then* Genesis is wrong in all its genealogies because it
> reports men living for nine hundred years or more.

If the conventional, old-age model of origins is true—
> *Then* Genesis (and other places in Scripture) got it wrong
> when it spoke about a global flood in the days of Noah.
> (The old-age model must deny a worldwide flood.)

If the conventional, old-age model of origins is true—
> *Then* Genesis (and the rest of the Bible) got it wrong when
> it claims that death entered the world as a result of the sin
> of Adam. (The old-age model must accept the presence of
> death and suffering and catastrophe for millions of years
> before man came on the scene.)

The reasons listed above and many other observations we could make would challenge the authority of Scripture and God as truth. You bet it matters!

What's Next?

We have seen something of the God Who is the Great Communicator, Who provides us with an eyewitness to Creation, and Who is Truth. We see Him as One Who is King of Creation, Who commands and it is done. We see the Artist as One Who creates with an appearance of age and challenges us to believe what we can't see because He requires those who come to Him to have faith that He is and that He is the Creator.

Next we will follow the events of Creation Week and look at the creation of the heavens (Creation Astronomy). What do we learn about the universe because we know something about the Artist Who created it? And what do we see in the universe that helps us to know more about the Artist?

Consider the Concept

When God creates something instantaneously, it often has the appearance of a process that took a great deal of time.

Questions to Ponder

- As you know by now, this book takes a "young-age" view of origins. If another believer challenges you concerning the age of things, how would you present to him the *biblical* case for Creation in six days? (Many points are given in the first half of the chapter.)
- Read the Gospel of John 2:1–10. The head waiter of the wedding feast very naturally assumed that the wine that Jesus created was old, made by natural processes. But actually the wine was instantaneously created. Were there any signs the waiter failed to observe that might have helped him to see the truth? Was there an eyewitness? How can you apply this story to the broad picture of God's creation of the world?
- Several considerations were given in the chapter that challenge the conventional way of thinking about the earth and universe as very old. Choose one that seems most compelling to you.
- Does age really matter? Review the last section of the chapter, where this question is discussed. Now explain to a fellow believer why age matters.

A Verse to Remember

For the LORD *made the heavens and the earth, the sea, and everything in them in six days; then He rested on the seventh day. Therefore the* LORD *blessed the Sabbath day and declared it holy.*

Exodus 20:11

Part 2

Creation Week:
What the Artist Has Made

Introduction

In part 2, we will follow the events of Creation Week. Chapters 4 to 7 will discuss the creation of the heavens, earth, living things, and mankind. What can we learn about these physical realities because we know something about the Artist Who created them? Conversely, what can we learn about the Artist from these incredible creative acts? Finally, what difference does it make in our lives to know these things?

Courtesy of NASA-Visible Earth

CHAPTER 4
GOD CREATED THE HEAVENS

AS our student, Scott, continues his search for understanding about God and His creation, his eyes naturally look above, to the universe. The beauty and wonder of the universe declare the glory of God to anyone who has eyes to see. However, Scott has also been conditioned, through many years of exposure, to assume the "Big-Bang" origin of the universe. That scenario of origins conflicts with what he has read in Genesis. How can it be that Genesis clearly states that the stars, sun, and moon were created on Day 4—after the light had appeared and after plants had appeared? Other perplexing questions arise when contemplating the size of the universe and the time required for light to travel from distant galaxies.

Considering the heavens leads one to other thoughts as well. Perhaps you have seen a popular poster of the universe that has appeared on walls in public places and in magazines. On it we see a photo of the universe, with its many galaxies. Also on the poster is a tiny dot. Beside the dot is a sign that says, "You are here." How insignificant that photo makes us seem! That poster supports the position of many atheists who cry out that man is an accident of evolution, totally inconsequential in a totally irrelevant universe.

First Priority: Consider God's Word

Yet, is that *really* what the universe teaches us? Is that interpretation of the universe consistent with the truth revealed in Scripture? No indeed! In Scripture we learn that the universe is a creation of the

When we consider the universe from this vantage point, how insignificant we must be!   Courtesy NASA-HST

Master Artist. Furthermore, we learn that the Artist created the entire universe with man central in His mind and design.

Can that really be so? Do we deceive ourselves when we make that claim?

Look for a moment at Psalm 8:3–6 on the next page. It begins by declaring that God's glory is even higher than the heavens. Then it goes on to describe what we experience when we look at the night sky and are overwhelmed with God's glory, sensing our insignificance in the light of it. However, it tells us that we are *not* insignificant, that in God's eyes we have been crowned with glory and honor. We have been given charge of all of the created order.

There are many other indications in Scripture of the worth God has placed on mankind. The ultimate proof of all, of course,

> **PSALM 8:3–6**
>
> *When I observe Your heavens, the work of Your fingers,*
> *the moon and the stars, which You set in place,*
> *what is man that You remember him,*
> *the son of man that You look after him?*
> *You made him little less than God*
> *and crowned him with glory and honor.*
> *You made him lord over the works of Your hands;*
> *You put everything under his feet.*

is that God Himself, in the form of His Son, became a man to bring us salvation.

Like any artist, God—the Master Artist—creates in order to bring glory to Himself. And He creates man in a universe that will enable us to know Him and bring glory to Him. In the remainder of this chapter we will look at some of the physical evidence found in the universe and how God's nature is revealed in the things He has made.

> **PSALM 19:1**
>
> *The heavens declare*
> *the glory of God,*
> *and the sky proclaims the*
> *work of His hands.*

Physical Evidence: The Anthropic Principle

The Anthropic Principle is an interesting set of observations about the universe. In fact, it was actually discovered and proposed by unbelieving scientists. The Anthropic Principle is the observation that *the universe* looks *as if it was created for man*. It is incredibly "fine-tuned" in order to maintain life. Of course, many scientists and others deny what God is shouting and conclude that it couldn't really be true; it only *appears* to be true.

However, we Christians know that God has created the universe for man so that humans can live and come to know Him. Let's look now at a few of the many observations in the universe that make it look as if it was created for man.[1]

God Created Natural Laws and Processes

There are laws—physical laws—in the universe that seem to operate at all levels. The consistent operation of these rules is what allows us to exist. If there were no such regularities, if things randomly changed around all the time, we couldn't exist.

For example, we rely on space being here tomorrow; otherwise, we would wake up and disappear.

We assume gravity isn't going to change tomorrow, or we would fly out of our beds and never come back.

Our bodies are constructed of particles of physical matter in three-dimensional space. In order for our bodies to operate reliably, they must be made of particles with a consistent nature, they must work according to consistent patterns, and space must hold these particles together in a consistent manner. (If this weren't true, picture yourself scattered across the universe as trillions of particles!)

Another example of the rule-based nature of the physical world is the three dimensionality of the universe. Have you ever witnessed some of the sci-fi speculations about what would happen if the universe were two dimensional (like a piece of paper), or even four dimensional? Those who have thought more about these things than we have concluded that life as we know it on earth can only exist in three dimensions.

Consider also one of the constants of the universe: electromagnetic force. Electromagnetic force is that force that attracts positive and negative charges. It is *essential* for our existence. However, even more critical to our existence is how *strong* it is. It cannot be much stronger or weaker, or we wouldn't live. If it were a little weaker, then the electrons that are held around the nucleus by electromagnetic force would "zing" off into space, leaving no electrons around the nuclei. Without electrons, there would be no possibility of sharing electrons to make molecules. Without molecules, life wouldn't be possible. On the other hand, if the force were just a little stronger, then the electrons would be held firmly in place, never moving off the nucleus. They would never be shared with another atom. If electrons were never shared, molecules could not form. As it "happens," electromagnetic force is exactly the right strength to allow life to exist. Coincidence?

Master Design Seen in Every Particle of the Universe

God's consideration of man shows up in the design of the entire universe—from its most basic structure to the largest bodies it contains. Consider the following examples:

- *Atomic Level: The Carbon Atom.* Most of the molecules in the human body are built upon a backbone of carbon atoms. God designed the carbon atom to have particular characteristics that make it ideal for organic molecules.
- *Molecules: Carbon Dioxide.* As a gas, carbon dioxide is made available to plants in abundance, and its greenhouse effects allow comfortable temperatures on the earth's surface. When dissolved in water, carbon dioxide produces carbonic acid, another important molecule in the erosion of rocks and the sustaining of acidic solutions. This molecule is absolutely essential for human life to exist and flourish.
- *Water: Another Remarkable Molecule.* Water is truly a spectacular substance! Not only is it the most abundant single molecule in the human body; it also has some amazing characteristics that make it a great place for the processes of life to occur.

    1. Many substances can be dissolved in water.

    2. Water is a liquid at normal temperatures on the earth's surface, so it makes a good fluid for transporting molecules.

    3. Contrary to most substances that expand as they are heated, water actually expands as it freezes. This allows ice to float. If water acted like other substances in the universe, frozen water would sink and lakes would freeze from the bottom up, making life in water in cold regions impossible.

    4. Water has the tendency to "stick" to itself. This causes it to form droplets. This characteristic permits insects, such as water striders, to walk on top of water. More importantly, it permits water to be pulled long

distances through tubes of small diameter, thus permitting trees to draw water many feet upward to their leaves.

5. Water's unique ability to carry large amounts of heat, especially when evaporating, permits water to function as an air-conditioning fluid.

- *Our Earth's Position in Space.* The earth is 8,000 miles in diameter and weighs roughly 6.6×10^{21} tons. It travels a 292-million-mile orbit around the sun. If the earth traveled much faster, centrifugal force would pull it away from the sun, and if it was pulled away too far, all life would cease. If the earth rotated more slowly on its axis, all life would eventually die, either by freezing at night because of lack of heat from the sun or by burning during the day from too much sun.
- *Our Galaxy and Beyond.* Within our own Milky Way galaxy, God made sure that stars were not placed close enough to our solar system to pull planets out of their orbits. God designed our solar system with a single star (unlike most, which have multiple suns) so the earth's orbit was stable. Of all the different types of stars in the universe, our star's color was chosen for photosynthesis and its type was chosen for stability. He arranged moons around planets. Beyond our own galaxy, we see incredible organization. God arranged galaxies into galactic clusters and galactic clusters into superclusters.

More Physical Evidence: The Second Law of Thermodynamics

The Second Law of Thermodynamics is one of the laws of the universe, one of those regularities we observe consistently in the world around us. Let's try a simple explanation for this very complicated discipline of science.

Thermodynamics is fundamentally an issue about heat (*thermo*=heat; *dynamics*=movement); it is all about heat motion. To oversimplify: when you have a bunch of hot stuff over here and cold stuff over there, the hot stuff tends to go over to where the cold stuff is and even out the heat.

So what are the consequences of this heat transfer? One is that that which is complex will tend to become less complex with time. Consider a beautiful new car; it becomes rusty and eventually wears out. And how about that room your mother just cleaned so nicely? Even on its own, without your help, it will become dusty and moldy. The Second Law of Thermodynamics says that all systems that are closed will break down; in other words, all systems that don't have energy coming in from the outside will break down and become less and less complex.

But we all know of some systems that become *more* complex with time. For example, a seed grows into a tree. A fertilized egg grows into an adult human. A complicated building can be made from bricks, mortar, and other seemingly simple materials.

In order to reverse the Second Law's consequences, we have consistently observed that three things seem to be necessary.

1. A Source of Energy. In a factory, we have electricity coming in. When we build a building, a bunch of workers supply the energy for the building process. The tree has light coming in to supply the needed energy. In your room, you or your mother supply the energy necessary to reverse the disorder that is inevitable from the Second Law.

But energy is not enough. If we have a pile of materials that will ultimately be made into a building, it isn't enough to simply let the sun beat down on those materials, providing energy to build the building. Something more is needed.

2. An Energy Converter. You must be able to put the energy into the proper form. The tree requires the incredible system of photosynthesis to take the energy from the sun and put it into the proper form. The one who builds the building needs electric machinery to convert electric energy into forms that cut lumber, lift beams, seal pipes, etc. Builders themselves must have a digestive system and a complex body to convert food energy into necessary body movement. In every instance where there is a reversal in the Second Law of Thermodynamics, not only is there energy coming in from the outside, but there seems to be an energy converter to put it into useful form.

3. A Blueprint. Finally, an organized plan seems to be needed. You can feed people and they will have all the energy they need because they have all the machinery inside their bodies to convert it into usable form. But even if they were then given bricks, mortar, steel, and tools, they probably wouldn't be able to construct a building. They need a blueprint and training. They need an intelligent plan. Even trees need DNA information to put the energy to proper use.

Second Law of Thermodynamics

In a closed system, any complex organization of energy, matter or information will become less complex over time.

Three things are necessary to stop or reverse the process: 1. A source of energy from outside; 2. an energy converter; and 3. a blueprint or plan of action.

Over time, a silver spoon will tarnish badly.

Energy and someone, who is cleaning the spoon, results...

In a rollback of the 2nd Law and a clean spoon!

Erkel and Associates (Crozet, Va.)

Conclusion. Now, let's apply what we've learned about the Second Law of Thermodynamics to the universe and to the nature of God. First of all, complexity in systems tends to decrease with time if there is no external energy source, a proper energy conversion mechanism, and a design. Therefore the greatest complexity would have to be at the beginning. But where did this complexity come from? What we have discussed about the Second Law of Thermodynamics would suggest that the universe's energy has an external energy source, that something is capable of converting that energy into usable form, and that some sort of intelligent plan was followed. In other words, *whatever caused the universe was both very powerful and very intelligent.* Whatever caused the universe had more energy than the total amount of energy in the entire universe, *and* it was able to control all the energy of the universe. In essence, the cause of the universe had *all power* (it was *omnipotent*). In addition, the information possessed by the cause of the universe must have been greater than the total amount of information placed into the universe. This would suggest that the cause of the universe had more information than is found in the universe—meaning that it had *all knowledge* (it was *omniscient*). Does that sound like Someone you know?

Compelling Evidence: The Artist Reveals Himself in the Things He Has Made

We looked at Romans 1 in chapter 1 of this book. Let's look at it again. Verse 20 explains that God designed the creation in such a way that people can clearly see His invisible qualities—His eternal power and His divine nature. Since He requires faith of us, He does not go so far as to provide proof that He is Creator. Compelling evidence, yes; proof, no. The very structure of the universe provides compelling, nonproven evidence of God and His nature.

> **ROMANS 1:20**
>
> *From the creation of the world His invisible attributes, that is, His eternal power and divine nature, have been clearly seen, being understood through what He has made. As a result, people are without excuse.*

- *God is the first cause.* By definition the physical universe contains all matter, space, and time. Can you imagine being around *before* there was matter, space, and time? God was. The Cause of the universe had to be independent of matter, material space, and time. Therefore, It must have been nonphysical (not made of matter). Since the Cause was independent of space, the Cause must have been independent of space both outside the universe (transcendent) and at every place within the universe (immanent, everywhere present). Since It was independent of physical time, the Cause must have been unchanging, always present, and eternal. The Artist God—the Creator of the universe—is nonphysical, transcendent, immanent, unchanging, always present, and eternal.
- *God loves variety.* Because He is a Trinity, even His internal nature is diverse. He loves variety. So when He created the bodies of the universe, He created great variety. He created different kinds of galaxies and a variety of stars. He created a variety of planets, moons, and comets. This variety has been difficult to explain in atheistic origins models.
- *God is abundant.* The universe was created larger than it had to be and with a greater variety of astronomical bodies than was necessary to accomplish His purposes.
- *God loves beauty.* The universe is incredibly beautiful. The planets and their moons, the galaxies and their stars are majestic in their brilliance. Their beauty stimulates awe in humans and declares the glory of God.
- *God loves order.* Modern science discovered a principle of symmetry in the universe. An illustration: the Periodic Table of chemistry. Once chemists discovered enough elements to determine a pattern in the table, they were able to then predict the nature of other elements to complete the table. The principle of symmetry has been used to predict the existence and characteristics of subatomic particles. Even the forms of the natural laws of the universe are elegant.[2]

Indeed, the heavens declare the glory of God (Psalm 19:1) and shout to us Who He is.

A Case Study: The Big Bang

What Is It?

The Big Bang plays well on university campuses. Even when a person knows nothing at all about astronomy, he can usually be counted on to hold the assumption that somehow the Big Bang is responsible for the universe coming into existence. Christians expend much effort trying to make the theory somehow "fit" the Bible. It leaves God totally out of the picture, yet we believers valiantly try to find a place for Him.

Let's put our principles into practice as we help our student, Scott, look at this idea about how the universe came into being. If you have had some physics, you will be able to follow the description below. If not, feel free to omit this part of the chapter and move on.

First, Scott must understand the claims of the Big-Bang hypothesis. It goes something like this: At the beginning of time, all the space, matter, and time of the universe was compressed into infinite or near-infinite density (compactness). It began to expand from there. Very early in its expansion, energy in the form of very high-energy gamma radiation condensed into subatomic particles, most of which collided again to produce gamma rays. As the expansion continued, however, the gamma rays became stretched. Once stretched so far, they lacked the energy necessary to produce more subatomic particles. But the density and temperature for a time was high enough to fuse heavy particles together to produce atomic nuclei. This continued until the expansion had dropped temperatures and pressures below what was needed for fusion.

During this entire period, the universe's particles were so close together that light could not travel very far before it bounced off them. Not until the expansion separated the particles far enough could the light become free to travel through the universe. Traveling in every direction because of earlier collisions, the light moved ever afterward, going in all directions into space. Billions of years of expansion since this event stretches the original gamma radiation into microwaves. Evidence of such a beginning of the universe would be found: (1) in the large ratio of particles of light to particles of matter, (2) in light elements in abundances inversely proportional to their mass, and (3) in microwave radiation coming in uniformly in all directions. Because each of these expectations is known to be true of our universe, the Big-Bang theory is well evidenced. Because the microwave radiation was a prediction of the theory even before it was possible to detect such radiation, the Big-Bang theory is even more powerfully supported.

Why Not the Big Bang

Case closed? No, the next step for any inquiring student is to ask: "Is the Big Bang true *biblically?*" It cannot be true for the following reasons:

1. According to Scripture, the universe is only about six thousand years old; the Big-Bang theory requires it to be billions of years old. (Exodus 20:11—"For the LORD made the heavens and the earth, the sea, and everything in them in six days.")

2. Subatomic particles, the elements, and many of the compounds of the universe were created in a single day of Creation Week; the Big-Bang theory has these things developing over billions of years.

Second, Scott must look at the data and determine whether or not the assumptions made are consistent with the data. When this is done, a few observations follow:

1. The Big Bang assumes that the matter of the universe is uniformly distributed. That something is wrong with the Big-Bang theory is evidenced by the fact that the microwave radiation has actually been found to be *too* uniform—more uniform than the distribution of matter in the universe.

2. The Big-Bang theories include the unboundedness of the universe and its uniform distribution of matter. The uni-

verse must have no boundary. Yet Scripture seems to infer that there is a boundary to the universe. On the fourth day of Creation Week, God placed the sun, moon, and stars within the firmament (space, or expanse) of the heavens (Genesis 1:14–18). Two days earlier He had placed this firmament in order to separate "the waters above" from the waters below the expanse (Genesis 1:6–8). There are many different explanations of just what is being referred to by "the waters above." When the passage is carefully considered, there is a strong suggestion that all the bodies of the universe are bounded above by "waters above." If so, the universe is bounded, and this basic assumption of the Big Bang is invalid.

Other critiques of the hypothesis are available through a study of the literature. It is clearly a theory of men, and since it eliminates God from His creative work, it will ultimately fall.

Finally, the student needs to ask: "Are there other ways to interpret the data that are accurate and consistent with the stated truths of Scripture?" Yes, there are, although this work is in its infancy. (For a good summary of the state of creationist astronomy, see "The Current State of Creation Astronomy" by Danny Faulkner.)[3]

What's Next?

What do we learn about the earth beneath us from God's Word and from observations about the earth itself?

Consider the Concept

A person who has a biblical understanding and appreciation of the universe will also possess a strong sense of self-worth.

Questions to Ponder

- When you hear the Big Bang presented as fact on campus or in your church, how might you thoughtfully (and gently) respond?

- In this chapter you learned about the Anthropic Principle. What is it? Discuss at least one point given in the chapter that demonstrates this principle.
- What does Romans 1:20 teach about the character of God?
- Review what the chapter has to say about the Second Law of Thermodynamics. Now try to explain the law to someone and tell what this law teaches about God.
- God's Word has much to say about astronomy. Look up the following Scriptures and prepare to explain to a nonbeliever what the Bible teaches about the universe: Genesis 15:5; Nehemiah 9:6; Job 9:8–9; 22:12; Psalm 8:1, 3; 19:1; 33:6; 147:4; Isaiah 40:22, 26; 45:18; Jeremiah 10:12; 31:35, 37; 32:17; Colossians 1:16–17; Hebrews 11:3.
- Did you read anything in this chapter that you did not previously know, that you found exciting? Choose a principle/concept/fact that interested you, one you might find helpful to know in the future. Discuss or share it with someone.

A Verse to Remember

The heavens declare the glory of God,
and the sky proclaims the work of His hands.

                                         Psalm 19:1

CHAPTER 5
GOD CREATED THE EARTH

THE saga continues for our student, Scott, and all who seek truth regarding the origin of things. It is relatively easy to see the Creator in the universe, but now Scott's eyes look down to the pile of dirt and rock on which he is standing. What can that teach about the Artist?

Questions and challenges to faith arise when the discipline of geology is studied. The science of geology is a relatively young discipline, beginning in earnest during the nineteenth century when the philosophy of naturalism was becoming popular. As a result, the conventional approach to geology is saturated with naturalistic ideas and contradictions to biblical teaching. In geology class, Scott is taught to equate layers of rock to eons of earth history. The fossils are depicted as evidence of evolution from a common ancestor. Where is

Courtesy NASA-Visible Earth

God's place in earth history? Can the Bible be reconciled to what
the rocks are purported to show?

First Priority: Look to God's Word

Scripture tells us that God laid the foundations of the earth—
even before He created the universe, moon, and stars (see Genesis
1:9–19). That statement flies in the face of all that conventional science assumes. His Word also affirms
God's absolute control over what He
created. He controls rain, winds,
earthquakes, and volcanoes. His wisdom and might is revealed in this
creation. He is exalted in all His
works in founding the earth.

> **PSALM 24:1**
>
> *The earth and everything in it,
> the world and its inhabitants,
> belong to the LORD.*

Biblically, it is very difficult to know for certain about the earth
as it was originally created because the Fall and the Flood drasti-
cally changed that world. Many questions concerning rocks and
fossils will be addressed in the chapters on the Flood that come
later in this book. For now, we will focus on God's creation of the
physical world. We know that God had man in mind when He created, and God also knew this creation would need to endure for a
long time. What was the physical world like when it was originally
created?

Physical Evidence:
God Gave Us Solid Ground for Survival

Consider in the paragraphs that follow some of the observations of the Creator's design for man's habitat:

- *Proper Climate.* In addition to being placed in the best possible orbit about the sun, the earth was also placed at the
  proper tilt and given the proper rotational rate.
- *Proper Atmosphere.* In order to provide humans, animals,
  and plants the atmospheric gases they need (like water,
  oxygen, and carbon dioxide), the earth was created with
  enough mass so that its gravity can hold on to those

needed gases; yet it is not so massive that it also holds on
to the lighter, poisonous gases, such as hydrogen and
helium. And much more is involved. Think about the following observations of our atmosphere:

    1. The upper atmosphere chemistry destroys
    methane and ammonia, gases that can mess up
    organic chemistry and prove fatal if they exist in
    abundance.

    2. There is enough oxygen in the earth's atmos-
    phere to enable animals on land and in the sea to
    breathe, but not so much that forests would erupt
    spontaneously in flames.

    3. There is enough carbon dioxide in the atmos-
    phere to allow photosynthesis in plants, yet not so
    much that when combined with other greenhouse
    gases (water vapor, carbon dioxide, oxygen, and oth-
    ers), it would make the earth's atmosphere too warm.

    4. There is enough ozone in the atmosphere to
    protect the earth's surface from harmful ultraviolet
    radiation.

- *Magnetic Field Protection.* In order to provide protection
  from deadly charged particles coming in from the sun,
  the earth was created with a strong magnetic field.
  Because it was probably created with a strength sixteen to
  thirty-two times its present strength, the original magnetic field of the earth was probably also strong enough
  to prevent the creation and accumulation of radioactive
  Carbon-14. This magnetic field was probably formed by
  creating a large array of electrons circling the center of
  the earth. For these electrons to move in consistent circular orbits, the earth was created with a zone that is highly
  conductive electrically. This resulted in a threefold division of the earth's interior: an inner zone (called the
  inner core), a zone where the electrons circulate (called
  the outer core), and an outer zone (called the mantle).

Additionally, the mantle was created with a consistency that allows the crust to float on top of it.

- *Continents and Oceans.* By the end of Day 3 of Creation Week, the earth had continents and oceans. These are caused by differences in the rocks beneath. The upper three to five miles of rock beneath the ocean basins is called ocean crust. The upper twenty miles of rock beneath the continents is called continental crust. Since ocean crust is denser than continental crust, it floats lower in the mantle, just as oak wood floats deeper in water than balsa wood. It is probably no accident that at least three-fourths of the surface of the earth is covered by water, since the water-to-land ratio on the earth is critical in maintaining optimal surface temperatures.

We can't say for certain where the original continents were located at creation. Genesis 1:9 speaks of the waters being gathered together in one place to let the dry land appear. We can't really say if this is referring to a single ocean or a single land mass. It is obvious that there has been a great deal of continental movement in the past, and as we will see in a later chapter, reports of a single supercontinent known as Pangaea are likely related to Flood and post-Flood activity and don't reflect the way things were created. But we do know that God loves diversity and variety, so it should not be surprising that the original continents differed in shape, position, and topography.

The oceans were created as an environment for sea creatures, and that meant they must have contained the optimal balance of nutrients, minerals, and salt. Many different sediments would have been created on the ocean bottom, since not all organisms on the bottom of the sea live on rock. Then there is the consideration of proper pH: large volumes of lime mud were probably formed, for example, to help maintain the proper pH in the ocean. As on land, cycles were created for the continuous provision of nutrients and minerals. This probably involved both algae and oceanic bacteria, which were probably created on Day 2 or Day 3, with the oceans.

- *Lakes and Rivers.* These also would have had to be created with the bottom sediment and nutrients necessary to support the aquatic organisms that would live there.
- *Plants, Soil, and Bacteria.* We know that plants were created to serve as food for animals and man on Day 3, and those plants would need a lot of things: soils that were stocked with minerals and a water cycle to provide needed water. Even lightning plays an important role in the maintenance of quality soil on the present earth; therefore, lightning activity on the original earth was probably created to optimize early soils. Soils also needed to be created in various stages of formation, with all the processes of soil formation already in place. Since most of the cycles of the earth involve bacteria, it is possible that terrestrial (land) bacteria and maybe fungi were created on Day 2 in association with the earth before the creation of land plants.[1]

The Portrait of the Artist in the Earth He Created

We see God's omniscience (all knowledge) in the creation. God knew that man would sin. He knew that He would have to curse the entire creation and that He would have to judge the earth with a global flood. He knew what sinful man would do to His creation, so He created the earth with the remarkable ability to survive. We can observe today how the earth survives in spite of abuse.

We see His wisdom in the intricate design and interrelated nature of cycles in the earth system.

We see His love and provision in how the earth provides for the needs of the creatures that swim, fly, and crawl on its surface and how it is capable of surviving catastrophic judgments.

We see His love for mankind in how the earth is designed with man in mind.

We see His triune nature in the variety of continents, living environments, and ecosystems on the earth.

We see His abundance in the variety and beauty and complexity that exceeds what is necessary for organisms to survive.

We see His unity in the interrelated nature of the earth's systems.

We see His glory in the beauty of the earth.

What's Next?

Our student's eyes can clearly see the Creator and can conclude with the psalmist that "the earth and everything in it, the world and its inhabitants, belong to the LORD" (Psalm 24:1). Next, the picture broadens as our focus turns to living things—to the things God created "after their kind."

Consider the Concept

God created the earth with a remarkable ability to survive what He knew sinful man would do to abuse it.

Questions to Ponder

- What does the Bible say about the beginnings of the earth that contradicts conventional geological theory? What do you need to do when you are taught theory that conflicts with Scripture? How would you handle this (practically) in your geology class?
- Why is it difficult to know what the earth as originally created by God was like?
- God's Word has much to say about geology. Look up the following Scriptures and prepare to explain to a non-believer what the Bible teaches about the earth: Genesis 1:9–10; Job 5:10; 9:6; 37:6; Psalm 24:1–2; 68:5–9; 77:18; 89:11; 90:2; 102:25; 104:32; 115:16; 147:7–8; Isaiah 45:12; Haggai 2:6.
- Did you read anything in this chapter that you did not previously know, something you found exciting? Choose a principle/concept/fact that interested you, one you

might find helpful to know in the future. Discuss or share it with someone.

A Verse to Remember

Before the mountains were born,
before You gave birth to the earth and the world,
from eternity to eternity, You are God.

Psalm 90:2

Erkel and Associates (Crozet, Va.)

CHAPTER 6
GOD CREATED LIVING THINGS— AFTER THEIR KIND

AS Scott begins his biology classes at the university, he immediately encounters what is often said to be the "central theory of modern biology"—Darwinism. Evolutionary interpretations permeate every area of study. Furthermore, the explanations given often seem persuasively powerful. There is an evolutionary explanation for everything! Scott's professors confidently declare: "There is no evidence against evolution. There is no controversy over whether evolution took place, except from those who have religious reasons for it."[1] Once more Scott finds himself under attack, and doubts creep in. How can so many intelligent people who have studied biology so many years be wrong? What should Scott's next step be in resolving the dilemma?

First Priority: What Does God's Word Say?

Genesis 1 presents the fundamental framework for our understanding. We see that God created all the animals on the fifth and sixth days of Creation Week. He didn't begin with a single-celled creature that eventually diverged into many different forms; rather, He created specific groups, called "kinds," all during the same time frame. "After its/their kind" is repeated ten times in the first chapter of Genesis and is found elsewhere in Scripture as well. In the New Testament, Paul also comments in 1 Corinthians 15:39 about different kinds of "flesh." It does not seem possible to conclude "one common ancestor" from these passages.

Second, we can infer that the organisms He created in the beginning were fully formed and functional in adult form. The "chicken or egg" question was answered in Genesis 1.

We also observe that a particular order was followed: plants and trees were created on the third day; sea creatures and birds on the fifth day; and cattle, beasts of the earth, creeping things, and man on the sixth day. This order is directly contradictory to modern evolutionary theory.

In addition, we discover that evolutionary theory challenges the character of God in its assertion of random, purposeless forces; violence; and death—all elements that are required by the theory.

What then should Scott, our Christian student, do in light of the blatant contradictions he sees between the Word of God and the interpretations of men? Once again, he needs to reaffirm his claim that Scripture presents absolute truth. As he goes on to examine the observations and data from the physical world, he should be challenged to seek an interpretation of the data that supports the truths of Scripture.

As Scott looks to the physical world expecting to see the Artist's hand, he will be delighted by what he observes. Job 12 says it well:

Ask the animals, and they will instruct you;
[ask] the birds of the sky, and they will tell you.
Or speak to the earth, and it will instruct you;
let the fish of the sea inform you.
Which of all these does not know
that the hand of the LORD has done this?
The life of every living thing is in His hand,
as well as the breath of all mankind.
(Job 12:7–10)

Physical Evidence: Consider the Animals

The theory of evolution is an elegant one. If Scott approaches his studies claiming that the theory is "stupid," he will later have great difficulty when faced with what may seem to be compelling evidence in its support. Although clearly (to a believer's eye) it is a false theory—a counterfeit to biblical revelation—it does contain some kernels of truth. Like most counterfeits, it has great explanatory power for those who have chosen to exclude God from their minds and lives. It even captures some believers because of its persuasive nature.

In this chapter we will introduce some evidences that point strongly to God's character and glory in His creation of living things—evidences that show that young-age creationism presents by far the most satisfying explanation for the life we see around us. This is a huge area of study, far beyond the scope of a single chapter or book. The following areas of study will be overviewed:

1. God is a Communicator: The language of DNA
2. God knows everything: The incredible complexity and design of living things
3. God loves abundance and variety: Baraminology—a biblical system of classification of living things
4. God's beauty
5. God's perfection
6. Summary: Why the young-earth interpretation is superior to the evolutionary interpretation

God Is a Communicator: The Language of DNA

The ability to communicate is a powerful indicator of intelligence. In the popular 1997 film *Contact,* the young woman scientist for the SETI project devoted her life to searching for patterns in the radio signals from space, patterns that indicated a form of communication. Intelligence in the form of extraterrestrial life was quickly inferred because communication, in the form of a mathematical language, was demonstrated.

God spoke the world into existence. He sent His Son (the living Word) to live and die for us. He gave us His written Word. He communicates through His created world. He made men and women able to communicate with one another and with God Himself. He is the Creator of all languages. Is it any wonder that the signature of His communication skills would be obvious even at the molecular level, in the marvelous molecule DNA, found in every cell in our bodies?

The "Great Array" of radio-astronomy telescopes in New Mexico. Those who search for extraterrestrial life look for signs of communication from space. Communication is a powerful indicator of intelligence. Courtesy of VLA-NRAO

DNA is a famous molecule. The familiar double helix appears on the cover of magazines and in both scientific and popular journals. It often plays a major role in courtroom dramas and on the front pages of newspapers. Considering the fact that it was only first described by Francis Crick and James Watson in 1953, it has swiftly risen to its position of importance.

DNA, found in the nucleus of the cell, contains the assembly instructions for the thousands of proteins that are the building blocks of life.

Let's examine more closely the language of DNA, using the English language as an analogy.

- *The English language has a code.* Twenty-six letters—arranged in particular lengths and orders—provide the codes for words. The words then string together as code for phrases and complete thoughts. *DNA also has a code.* A string of four different chemicals, called nucleotides, are referred to by their letters (**G**uanine, **C**ytosine, **A**denine, and **T**hymine). The four nucleotides are arranged in sequences of three (called *codons*) to code for the twenty or so amino acids used in living organisms. These codons are strung together in complex sequences (called *genes*) to code for the tens of thousands of proteins in the human body.

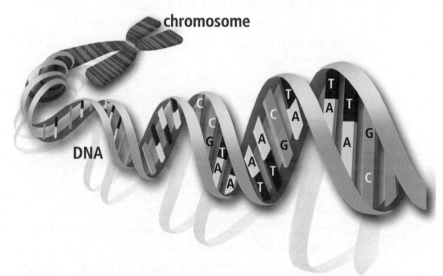

One of the ways we see DNA as a language is through its code letters GCAT. Just as letters of the English alphabet code for words, the nucleotide letters are used to code for tens of thousands of proteins in the human body.
Courtesy of U.S. Department of Energy, human genome project

- *The English language is modular. Modular* refers to a design with standardized units or dimensions that afford flexibility and interchangeability in use. We see modular bookcases, modular homes, and modular computer parts. Human language is also modular. Letters can be added to the beginning or end of words to change the meaning of the word. One prefix or suffix can be switched for another to change tenses of verbs, the plurality of nouns, etc. This flexibility also works at higher levels. Words can be substituted for other words in a sentence, phrases can be inserted or removed, paragraphs can be altered and rearranged. *DNA also shows this characteristic.* Since four different nucleotides in three positions could code for as many as sixty-four items, and yet codons in living systems only code for twenty or so, more than one individual codon is assigned to code for a given amino acid. This means that an interchange in the nucleotides can at times lead to no change in the protein. Other amino acid changes do significantly change the protein structure, but they create proteins of only slightly different function, somewhat like what a suffix or prefix change might have on a particular word. At another level, processing a gene in a slightly different way can produce a slightly different protein. At an even higher level, one gene can be substituted for another gene, resulting in a completely different protein being substituted for another. Genes can be turned off by other DNA sequences. There are even mechanisms to insert or delete genes. At a higher level, entire gene groups can be substituted for other gene groups by insertion, deletion, or by being turned on or off. This emergent modularity (complexity at different levels of organisms) in DNA allows extraordinary flexibility and the ability to code for a lot of complexity in a very compact length.

- *The English language has a linguistic structure.* Words are classified into categories such as nouns, verbs, adjectives, etc. There are rules that determine how the various categories of words relate to one another. For example, a preposition must be linked with an object of the preposition, an adjective must be linked with a noun, an adverb must be linked with a verb. Other linguistic rules define the order of words and phrases. All human languages possess their own linguistic structure. *In DNA there is also a hint of linguistic structure.* There are codon sequences that function in turning particular genes on or off. Other codon sequences change the rate at which a particular gene is used. Still other codon sequences modify multiple genes. There are also examples of particular groups of codon sequences that must be activated in a particular order before genes can be activated or turned off. There indeed seem to be rules that direct how codon sequences relate to one another.

- *The English language has a sending mechanism.* A thought must be expressed in order to communicate effectively; merely thinking it won't suffice. In English, that communication is through spoken or written words—something the receiver can understand and respond to. *DNA also needs to be read and understood.* Within the cell, the DNA is close-packed to save space, and it cannot be read in that form. Sophisticated mechanisms exist to unzip the DNA so it can be read. Furthermore, the information found in the DNA is needed outside the nucleus rather than inside, where most DNA is stored. Additional complex mechanisms are present that copy the information from the DNA onto specially designed molecules of messenger RNA that carry the information outside the nucleus in a form that can be used by the cell.

- *Finally, the English language needs a proper receiver.* A perfect English sentence will not be understood by one who understands only the Chinese language. A non-braille book will not be understood by a blind person. The receiver must be equipped with the ability to understand the information he or she is given. *In the case of DNA,* most of the cell cannot make sense of the information on the messenger RNA. Sophisticated machinery in the cell is devoted to translating messenger RNA information into chains of amino acids in proper sequence. These chains are folded in proper shapes and tagged for proper location by other mechanisms. They are then transported to the proper locations by still other mechanisms. Only then can these molecules be useful in allowing the cell processes to work.

DNA has the structure of language. All organisms on earth have DNA. Therefore evidence of language is found in all earth's organisms. Since God created with evidence of His nature, and since God is a communicating God, the language basis of organisms should not come as a surprise to creationists. However, noncreationists would not expect DNA to be based on something so complex as a language.

God Knows Everything: The Complexity of Living Things

God knows everything. When we look at the splendor and complexity of living things, we intuitively know that Someone much bigger than ourselves must be responsible. Be ready to absorb some mind-boggling information as we briefly consider the wonder of life.

Microscopic Creatures on Our Planet. Think for a moment about the simple, one-celled creatures whose existence most of us don't recognize until we look through a microscope in high school biology class. Some of these tiny organisms thrive in the water of your water heater, while others live in glacial ice. Some live in acid; others live on salt. Some forms eat oil, thriving thousands of feet beneath the earth's surface. Some of them get energy from the sun; some, from hydrogen gas; and some, from sulfur dioxide. And this only scratches the surface.

Most humans don't recognize that their very survival depends upon such one-celled critters. For example, humans and most animals cannot break down complex plant molecules. So the job of digesting most of the plant material in the world falls on the tiny, one-celled organisms in their intestines. In addition, animals and plants are unable to get the nitrogen they need for survival without the help of single-celled organisms that are capable of breaking the powerful bonds of nitrogen molecules in the atmosphere and ultimately producing nitrogen as a waste product. In fact, a myriad of elements we need to survive—phosphorus, sulfur, molybdenum, nickel, and on and on—are made available to us ultimately through the activity of the earth's bacteria.

Awesome Cell Structure. In Darwin's time, the cell was thought to be a rather nondescript blob of protoplasm. It was conceivable then that it could have rather easily evolved from nonliving chemicals on the primordial earth. My, how times have changed! College cell-biology students should have something to say about the conceivability of this idea, considering our current understanding of the cell.

A cell is like a gigantic factory containing a countless number of machines. Cell membranes surround the cell, providing protection and allowing only certain things in and out of the cell. Genetic information for repairs, reproduction, and the building of cellular structure is stored in DNA molecules. The more complex organisms pack their DNA tightly into specially designed chromosomes. In these more complex organisms, the region is protected with a specially designed membrane (to define a nucleus). Another region of the cell is devoted to producing ribosomes—the machines that construct amino acid chains from messenger RNA. Other regions of every cell are devoted to the folding and tagging of protein molecules. The more complex organisms cordon off those sections of the cell with membranes (endoplasmic reticulum and golgi bodies) to increase efficiency of production.

Every cell also has structures designed to extract energy from the environment. The more complex of the organisms concentrate the energy extraction in special structures surrounded by their own membranes and containing some of their own DNA. These include mitochondria (for extracting energy from glucose sugar) and chloroplasts (for extracting energy from sunlight).

And it gets even more complex. Each of the processes of the cell involves complex chemical reactions. The unwinding, unzipping, copying, rezipping, and rewinding of the DNA requires a complex set of chemical machinery. The process of modifying and transporting the messenger RNA to the ribosomes requires another complex set of chemical machinery. The creation of an amino acid chain, the folding of proteins, the tagging of proteins, the transport of proteins, the selection of molecules to be taken in and let out of the cell, and the processes of extracting energy from the environment—each of these require complex machinery. Further machinery is needed for the cell to assume and change its shape, to move, and to ingest items from outside the cell. The complexity, beauty, and elegance of these molecular systems are awesome and stunning.

Complex Core Design. While we are considering complexity, think also about how these various parts of the living machine must work together. In every machine there are parts that are absolutely necessary for that machine's function. These parts make up the "core design" of the machine. If any part of the core design is absent, the machine doesn't work. If any part of the core design is malfunctioning, the machine either doesn't work well or it doesn't work at all. Parts of the machine not in the core design can be added, taken away, or modified without crippling or stopping the machine's function. The more parts that are found in its core design, the more complex is the central design of the machine. The core design of even the simplest cells on earth are composed of a stunning number of parts—a complexity expected of an all-knowing and all-wise God. It is difficult to imagine how even this minimal complexity of life could arise naturalistically—without purpose, plan, or complex manipulation. Examples of complex core designs among many of life's molecular machines are given by Michael Behe in his book *Darwin's Black Box*.[2] He discusses how difficult it would seem to be to generate many of life's core designs (which he calls "irreducible complexity") by means of evolution. A nonliving example of this irreducible complexity is the common mousetrap. Behe describes the five parts of the mousetrap system: a base platform, a metal hammer, a spring, a catch that releases, and a metal bar that holds the hammer back. This, he continues, constitutes a core design because all parts must be present and functioning together to catch the mouse. It seems impossible for that mousetrap to "evolve" one step at a time.

We see complexity not only at the molecular level but at every level of biology. We find complex chemical systems within complex cells. We find cells in complex tissues and tissues within complex organs. Organs are located within complex organ systems and organ systems within complex bodies. Organisms are arranged in complex populations. Even communities and ecosystems are arranged on a global level so that carbon, sulfur, nitrogen, and phosphorus can be cycled through the earth's organisms for a continuous supply. All this without a Designer?

It really isn't too difficult for any of us to identify when something has been designed, even if we don't actually see the designer. When we see carved on a tree the words "John loves Mary," it would be highly unlikely to conclude this to be a result of time, chance, and natural processes. If you visited Mount Rushmore in South Dakota, you would see a mountain that shows the faces of some famous Presidents. Obviously, some intelligent and skilled designer had been at work. In Disney World you observe bushes that are shaped like Disney characters and animals. Is it likely they just happened to grow that way? If these kinds of things are so obvious, then it is almost inconceivable that we could look at living things and not see a Designer—One Who is intelligent beyond our wildest imagining. In fact, He made that design obvious so that we could marvel in His nature.

God Loves Abundance and Variety

One can never say that God is boring. Just look around His world; abundance is everywhere. Has it ever occurred to you, when you look at a spring hillside, how many shades of green there are? God could have created the world in black and white. He also could have created a generic sort of bird, but instead we have multitudes of species of every shape, color, and size. When He created fish, He allowed for such variety that there would be worlds of unimagined splendor deep below the ocean where men couldn't even go before the advent of deep sea diving techniques. On the genetic level He gave us far more information in our genes than we would ever need. Or consider flowers: there are thousands of species of orchids alone. Indeed, even on the physical level God gives abundantly beyond what we could ask or think (see Ephesians 3:20).

But how did we get such diversity and variety? Darwin introduced the concept of a "tree of life"—that all organisms are related. He said that over millions of years a beginning species evolved into two species, and those branched into other species. This branching continued until over the course of billions of years, all the species of earth in all their categories gradually arose.

A young-earth creationist accounts for the diversity, variety, and relatedness of life in a much different manner. Plants were created in a single day; animals, in only two days. They were probably created in mature populations, since it seems to be God's nature to create something instantaneously and to fulfill His function for it at the moment of creation. Since a wide diversity of organisms was created instantly, the original organisms on earth were not in any way related to one another. As time passed, only offspring would be related to their parents.

We see the often-repeated phrase "after its/their kind" written ten times in the first chapter of Genesis. This, and the fact that all plants and animals were created in only three days, suggests God created all the major types of organisms separately. Instead of a "tree of life," with all organisms diverging from a common ancestor, the creationist would speak of an "orchard," where each separately created group of organisms is represented by a separate tree. In the course of time, each tree, or created kind, would produce a myriad of variations on the group's core design, branching and branching again into groups and subgroups.

There is a lot of confusion among believers concerning the meaning of *species* and how it relates to God's creation. Those who mock creationist thinking refer to the many species today and imply that creationists believe God created all the species we know today in just a few days. Then they speak of how difficult it would have been for Adam to name that many organisms and how impossible it would have been for Noah to squeeze them on the ark.

The term *species* is usually defined as "naturally interbreeding populations of organisms that under natural conditions do not interbreed with other populations." The biblical term *kind* is a broader term than the term *species* used in modern classification.

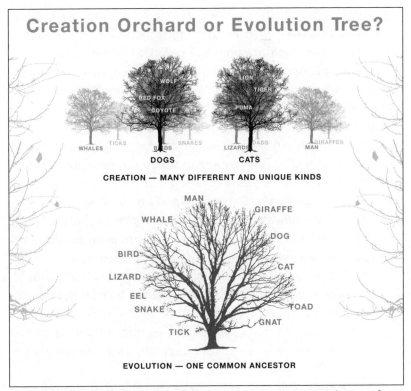

Creation Orchard or Evolution Tree?

WOLF
RED FOX
COYOTE

LION
TIGER
PUMA

WHALES   TICKS   BIRDS   SNAKES   LIZARDS   TOADS   MAN   GIRAFFES

DOGS   **CATS**

CREATION — MANY DIFFERENT AND UNIQUE KINDS

MAN
GIRAFFE
WHALE
DOG
BIRD
CAT
LIZARD
EEL
SNAKE
TOAD
GNAT
TICK

EVOLUTION — ONE COMMON ANCESTOR

The creationist speaks of an "orchard," where each separately created group of organisms is represented by a different tree. Darwin's "tree of life" claims that all organisms diverge from a common ancestor.   Erkel and Associates (Crozet, Va.)

Many fewer kinds were named by Adam and cared for by Noah than would be implied by the number of species known today.

Baraminology: In Search of the Created Kind. It is necessary for creationist biology to work out a classification system of its own because the current system of family/genes/species, etc., is based upon evolutionary theory and does not recognize what seems to be the biblical basis: the "created kind." A new and exciting field of creation biology is currently developing. It is called *baraminology.*

In Hebrew, the word for "created" is transliterated into English as *bara.* The Hebrew word for "kind" is *min.* Putting these words together, you get *baramin* or "created kind." The word was first coined in 1941 by Frank Lewis Marsh in a small book titled *Fundamental Biology*. In it he did something rather surprising for that day: he rejected the universal evolutionary tree. Instead, he suggested that God had created a number of "kinds" in the beginning, and from those original "kinds" our modern species have descended. We may then define a *baramin* as the organisms descended from the originally created "kind."

Marsh's baramin did not catch on for several decades, but recently a growing group of creationist scientists have begun working in earnest in establishing a classification that would have at its heart the original created kind. That field of study is called *baraminology*.[3]

How would one identify what creatures were in those original created kinds? The scope of this book does not allow for detail in this area, but the following will give you some idea:

- Scripture is our starting point. We know that the specific groups mentioned in Genesis 1 would define organisms that were never related. So, in verses 20–26 we read of birds, sea creatures, cattle, creeping things, beasts of the earth, and man. Each of these groups, then, contain separate baramins.

- Further division of these major groups into baramins is done by looking at *differences* among organisms—what is called *discontinuity* between the created kinds. Conventional evolutionary theory claims that all organisms are united. But discontinuities (breaks) seem to abound among living things and among fossils. These discontinuities help baraminologists to further identify the original created kinds.

  To name just a few, organisms that seem similar can have large differences in the machinery within the cell that copies their DNA. Some have differences in their genetic codes. Many organisms that seem similar have major differences in their metabolism, the way they obtain energy from their environment. Plants have many differences according to how they reproduce. Animals are divided according to how they reproduce and develop. It can all get very technical and detailed, but in short, young-age creationists expect (and evolutionists do not) evidence of unrelatedness abounding among the earth's organisms.

- These discontinuities between created kinds are also observed in the fossil record. Evolutionary theory requires that millions of transitions must have occurred to produce the many different kinds of organisms that exist and have existed in earth history. It is also believed that the fossil record has been preserving snapshots of earth history for billions of years.

If most species living in the present have a fossil record, and if species have persisted for millions to tens of millions of years, it is reasonable to expect that a fairly large percentage of the millions of transitional species between major groups that must have existed in the past would have been preserved in the fossil record. This, however, has not been the case. The rarity of transitional species between major groups in the fossil record seems to fit the expectations of young-age creationism better than the expectations of evolutionary theory.

This is especially evident among the shallow marine invertebrate (no backbones) animals. Something on the order of 95 percent of the fossil record consists of shallow water marine invertebrates. Yet there seems to be a complete absence of transitional species among these animals—even though these are the best-represented animals in the fossil record!

On a higher level of biological organization, the young-age creation model would also expect communities to appear suddenly in the fossil record since God created mature communities. The Flood may have buried some of these communities in their entirety. Both of these expectations should result in the sudden appearance of communities of organisms in the fossil record without much apparent development of those communities over time. This has proved to be the case: organismal communities do seem to appear suddenly in the fossil record—an observation difficult to explain in conventional evolutionary theory.

- When we identify baramins, we see many *differences* among organisms, but we also see many *similarities*—evidence that some organisms should be grouped together in the same baramin. Organisms that can successfully interbreed should be of the same created kind. Surprisingly (to evolutionists), crosses between species are very common. Dogs can interbreed successfully with wolves and coyotes. Though they are different species, they are obviously members of the same kind. In plants, thousands of interspecific (between different species) hybrids are known among orchids. Among the 149 species of anatids (ducks, swans, and geese) in the world, 80 percent are known to cross with other anatid species. Land snails as well as numerous birds and mammals show common crosses. Have you ever seen a cama—a cross between a camel and a llama? How about a guck—a cross between a goose and a duck? A liger—a cross between a lion and tiger? A zorse—a cross between a zebra and a horse?

Zorses . . . new animals but not new kinds. "Tigger" belongs to Camilla Muluotoga, from New Mexico, and is the name she gave to this cross between a horse and a zebra, known as a "zorse."
Courtesy
Camilla Muluotoga

If the created kind is a larger group than the species, young-age creationists might expect successful crosses between species to be common among organisms on earth. This discovery, however, would not be anticipated in evolutionary theory. Those who maintain that the earth is billions of years old suggest that most of the earth's species have been distinct for hundreds of thousands to millions of years. It should be a rare event (not common) for two populations to remain capable of interbreeding after being separated for many thousands of generations.

One noteworthy example is the cama—the cross between a camel and a llama. According to conventional dating, these two species have been separated for at least forty million years. The successful crossing of a llama and a camel suggests that their separation was much more recent than that. The fact that interspecific (between different species) hybridization is common among many of the organisms of the world suggests that life's diversity is probably only as old as the thousands of years that young-age creationism suggests.

God's Beauty

When we look at the heavens, we see God's glory. The same is true when we look at the life He has created. Our spirits soar as we observe life in the sea, with the fantastic colors of corals and fish. We sit in awe at the beauty of land creatures, from birds to butterflies to toads and bumble bees. We wish we could write beautiful poetry or paint pictures to capture the beauty of the flowers and trees. The beauty of the biological world testifies to the glory of its Creator.

However, biological beauty is challenging to explain in evolutionary theory. Organisms usually generate their beauty at some cost to the organism. Either complex chemical pigments are required or clever mechanisms are employed for the diffraction of light. Either way, energy is expended by the organism to create and maintain its beauty. This should not have happened in traditional evolutionary theory because only what is necessary for the organism's survival should occur. Most beauty doesn't seem to be necessary for survival; rather, it seems to fulfill a function beyond survival: to show the abundance and glory of God.

God's Perfection

You may have heard the statement "God didn't make no junk." Although grammatically incorrect, this is a profound statement. When God completed His creation after the sixth day, He pronounced it all "very good." The Hebrew words for "very good" don't mean simply a grade of "A-minus." Instead, they signify "the best it could possibly be." No mistakes. Perfection. Adam must have been awesome in his intelligence and beauty.

A young-age creationist would expect that mutations (mistakes in DNA copying) began after man messed everything up by his sin. We would conclude that mutational load (a measure of the total number of mutations, or mistakes, an organism carries) started out at zero and has grown to its present level only in the last few thousand years.

Other models of earth history suggest that organisms have been in existence hundreds of thousands of times longer than creationists propose. Along that line of reasoning, hundreds of thousands of times more mutations would have occurred. In that case, mutations have been accumulating for so many years that unless some mechanism for cleaning out mutations exists, all organisms would have died out long ago from catastrophic errors in their DNA. Yet organisms do not seem to be going extinct because of high mutational loads.

It is now becoming possible to measure the mutational load of organisms. The young-age creation model predicts that those loads will be much smaller than expected in conventional theory—small enough to suggest that life on earth has been here only for thousands of years, not millions or billions of years.

Summary

Scott's classroom study of biology has demonstrated some powerful evidence for evolution. Similar evolutionary trees are derived

from a study of organisms, their development, and their biochem-
istry as if they evolved according to the branching pattern suggested
by those trees. Organisms can be arranged in a hierarchy of increasingly large groups as if they were all derived from a common ancestor. Organisms have developed along trajectories similar to the path
of evolution they are thought to have traveled. Scott has seen that
evolutionary theory provides a simple explanation for these features of biology.

But . . .

Young-age creation theory explains the same features and *more*.
Although there is not room enough here to explain all these things
in detail, we will give an overview:

- It explains not just the fact that organisms can be
arranged in a hierarchy of increasingly large groups, but
also why there are so many characters that seem to contradict that pattern.
- It explains the similarities among organisms (used by evolutionists to argue for relatedness), but it also explains the
commonness of evidence for unrelatedness.
- It provides explanation for the incredible beauty of biology, the complexity that characterizes the earth's organisms, as well as the language structure of DNA.
- It explains the commonness of species that can interbreed, what seems to be a low mutational load in organisms, as well as the sudden appearance of organisms and
communities of organisms in the fossil record.
- It explains what evolutionary theorists call *embryological
recapitulation*—a theory that the stages of an organism's
development, from single cell to adult, look similar to the
stages in the evolutionary ancestry of that organism.
Young-age creationism can explain why the development
of the organisms often *broadly* looks like the hypothesized
evolution, but also how the examples break down when
examined in detail.[4]

- It explains what evolutionists call *suboptimal improvisations*—biological structures that appear to be examples of poor design (the Panda's thumb is one of just a few examples)—and why they are so uncommon.[5]

Even though young-age creation biology is in its infancy, there is reason to believe that it is at least comparable—and even now may be superior—to evolutionary biology in its explanatory power.

A Case Study: Similar Structures in Different Organisms (Homology)

Any textbook dealing with bioevolution will find space for a discussion of the many similar structures found in different organisms (called *homology*). One can enroll in "Comparative Anatomy" classes in college. Illustrations abound in the textbooks, for example, of the forelimbs of dogs, horses, monkeys, bats, penguins, and man. These serve to illustrate the common ancestry we all share. Since evolution is thought to be ongoing, the more recently two organisms shared a common ancestor, the more similar they ought to be. If all organisms did evolve via the "tree of life" from a common ancestor, these homologies can then be used to reconstruct that tree. Illustrations of the tree are also found in the textbooks. Therefore, since homologies are common and can be used to construct a treelike pattern of similarity, the assumption is made that all life evolved from some common ancestor.

Reasonable assumption? Yes.

Does it contradict Scripture? Yes.

Is there another way to interpret the data? You bet!

In young-age creation theory, God created all the various "kinds" of organisms. They were created with the capacity for substantial change. Because they were created by the same Designer, similar structures might be expected in similar positions (just as the same computer company makes similar keyboards for different computer models). A creationist, however, would *also* expect similar structures in different organisms, which contradict the idea of a *single* tree of life. Such tree-contradicting similarities (called homo-plasies) allow for the creation of *multiple* hierarchal trees.

Evidence? With the common use of computers in the last few decades, it has become possible to count how many different homology trees can be made and to count how many homo-plasies there are for each tree. These methods have shown that multiple trees and numerous homoplasies are the rule rather than the exception—just as young-age creation expects and evolution does not.

What's Next?

Creation Week reaches its climax on the sixth day with the cre-ation of mankind. This is where it gets personal: Who is man? What is his significance? How was he created?

Consider the Concept

The hand of the Creator is seen in the complexity, design, beauty, and variety of every living thing.

Questions to Ponder

- After reading this chapter, can you site any contradictions between evolutionary theory and the Word of God? Can you accept both as truth? If there is a contradiction, what do you need to do?
- You are a biology major. How can you (gently) confront the problems, both scientific and biblical, that you see in Darwinism and still remain a biology major?
- The marvelous molecule DNA was discussed at length. Name four or five things you learned about DNA that you didn't know before. What does DNA show you about its Creator?
- Complexity. It is mind boggling! Choose just one thing you learned about complexity of living things in this chapter that you didn't know. What does this tell you about the Artist?

- Evolutionary theory describes a "tree of life," while creationist theory uses the analogy of an orchard. Explain.
- What is a "baramin," and how does it differ from a "species"? What can the science of baraminology teach us?
- While evolutionary theory has some reasonable explanations for a number of biology's features, this chapter points out that young-age creation theory explains those features and more. See if you can remember one or two of the features that are *better* explained through understanding God as Creator.
- Read the following Scriptures that deal with the creation of living things. What do you learn from each? How could you summarize the passages to tell an unbeliever what the Bible teaches about the creation of living things? Genesis 1:20–25; Colossians 1:16; Proverbs 20:12; Psalm 50:10–11; Jeremiah 27:5; 1 Corinthians 15:39.

A Verse to Remember

Ask the animals, and they will instruct you;
[ask] the birds of the sky, and they will tell you.
Or speak to the earth, and it will instruct you;
let the fish of the sea inform you.
Which of all these does not know
that the hand of the LORD has done this?
The life of every living thing is in His hand,
as well as the breath of all mankind.

Job 12:7–10

CHAPTER 7
GOD CREATED MANKIND

UNIVERSITY life provides exposure to an extensive marketplace of ideas and the expression of those ideas. Free speech is an exciting principle, and the practice of free speech invites students to attach themselves to causes. As Scott continues his life at the university, he becomes aware of the smorgasbord of voices calling for his response. A casual walk around the campus on a beautiful fall day will encounter placards colorfully promoting twenty-first-century ideas: Save the Whales; Animals Are People Too; No Oil Drilling in Alaska; Abortion Is a Choice; The Right to Die; The Right to Live; Stop Capital Punishment; and Homosexual Rights (to name just a few).

Where does a Christian worldview fit into the clamor? Whose causes should Scott embrace? Should he merely withdraw and put his head into a Bible, or should he become involved? Believe it or not, a study of origins, particularly the subject of this chapter, gives clear direction to this concern.

Who *is* man? The story and circumstances of his origin are intimately related to his destiny and how he is to live his life.

First Priority:
What God's Word Tells about Man's Origin

Since we don't have any fossils of humans before the Fall or perhaps even before the Flood, and since no one living today has ever had a chance to personally know someone who has not suffered the effects of the Fall, we must look to Scripture to see what

Photo disc, Erkel and Associates (Crozet, Va.)

God considers important to tell us about His creation of man and His view of man. We can only speculate about some of the things we'd like to have answered. (Note: There will be some discussion about the "ape-men" and other fossils of man that are in the news today. Since these are all post-Flood fossils, we will deal with them in chap. 12.)

In this chapter we will focus on three observations about mankind as originally created by God. An understanding of these three principles will go a long way to helping Scott (and you the reader) sort out the validity of the various "causes" promoted in our culture. These principles are:

1. Adam and Eve (therefore, all men and women) were spe- cially created in God's image.
2. Adam and Eve were given a special mandate—"marching orders."
3. Adam and Eve, as created, were awesome!

A Special Creation: Created in God's Image

During Creation Week, God "spoke" the created things into being: the stars, the moon, the plants, the sea creatures, the land creatures, etc. But the creation of Adam and Eve was different—it was unique. We read of the Lord God forming man of the dust of the ground and breathing into his nostrils the breath of life. When He created Eve, He performed surgery! It is as if in these instances God "rolled up His sleeve and was willing to get His hands dirty." There was special, more intimate activity involved in this, His final creation.

Furthermore, He created man in His own image. Man is the only creation of God said to possess God's image. This reference to the image/likeness of God appears in a number of places in Scripture (Genesis 1:26, 27; 5:1; 9:6; 1 Corinthians 11:7; James 3:9). What does this *mean*? Anything mentioned that frequently in God's Word *must* be important.

Since God is spirit, we need not speculate that "image" means our physical characteristics are like God's. And it can't mean we have the characteristics of God's holiness, intelligence, etc. Even after man sinned, he is said to *still* reflect the image of God (although a marred image).

Furthermore, if the image of God were connected to physical characteristics (such as ability to reason, artistic ability, creativity, etc.), then the one who is born with brain damage, or the one who becomes disabled later in life, or the one who has not yet developed these things (such as the unborn) would then not have the image of God. In addition, most of the physical attributes of humans are found, at least in small measure, in various organisms. If the image of God were a physical thing such as intelligence, my dog might have more of the image of God than the child who has been brain damaged by encephalitis.

So perhaps the "image of God" has more of a *spiritual* orientation—for several reasons.

- Although man was created with the image of God, man is not supposed to create any physical images of God (Exodus 20:4). This suggests that image is more spiritual in nature.

- In the New Testament, the church is called the Body of Christ (Romans 12:5), yet it is not the physical bodies of believers that make up the church; the spiritual natures of the redeemed make up the spiritual Body of Christ.

- Since God is spirit (John 4:24), it stands to reason that a proper picture of Him would not be physical, but spiritual.

Some implications for having this "image of God" are spelled out in Scripture. In Genesis 9:6, following the Flood, we see that capital punishment was introduced as a response to murder because humans have the "image of God." We also see applications of this principle in the Mosaic Law. One of these applications is especially interesting (Exodus 21:22–25). According to this passage, if men were fighting and accidentally injured a pregnant woman, thereby causing injury to the unborn child, these men were to be punished "life for life, eye for eye, tooth for tooth, hand for hand, foot for foot, burn for burn, bruise for bruise, wound for wound."

(vv. 23–25). Since neither the stage of pregnancy nor the gender of the child is specified, it appears that an unborn child—male or female—is being equated part for part with an adult. This in turn suggests that the image of God is possessed by both men and women and is possessed by a child from the beginning of the mother's pregnancy—from the moment of conception!

A Special Mandate: The Dominion Mandate

In Genesis 1:26, God gave dominion over the creation to mankind: "They will rule the fish of the sea, the birds of the sky, the animals, all the earth, and the creatures that crawl on the earth."

Fallen man has abused this responsibility throughout the ages. What is the proper understanding of the dominion mandate? We tend to think of the man's dominion over the world as involving the justification for such things as eating animals, drilling for fossil fuels, or experimenting on animals to heal human diseases.

It is interesting to note that the dominion mandate was first given to Adam and Eve in the Garden of Eden. In that situation, the world was still perfect, with no death, disease, and suffering. Animals and man were initially vegetarian (Genesis 1:28–29). It was before most of the world's coal and oil were formed, and it was a time when all the resources for life were readily available. Since the needs of creation were probably totally supplied by God, it was not man's responsibility to provide things essential for creation's survival. So, what was there for Adam and Eve to do?

Since man was placed "in charge" of creation, it follows that he was charged to care for and nurture the creation beyond what the creation needed to persist. This is because God is a God of abundance. He did not just offer life; He offered a more abundant life. The original function of the dominion mandate was to enhance what the creation was already doing—to bring more glory to God.

Since the dominion mandate was delivered to the first created humans and is nowhere rescinded in Scripture, the dominion mandate is an obligation of all humans across all time. It remains an obligation for us today. The Fall of man introduced a number of new applications for the dominion mandate that were unknown in the pre-Fall world. But all fulfill the same purpose. Our obligation to the creation is to enhance the glory it brings to God. It is certainly not to abuse the creation or to consume it just because it is there and we are capable of ruining it.

Adam and Eve: An Awesome Creation!

Our society has conditioned us to think of humans as having evolved from an original, subhuman condition, with gradual increase in intellect and ability. This is certainly *not* the teaching of Scripture.

God created humans so they could glorify Him from the moment of their creation. Humans were created in mature form—with intelligence, language capacity, and language itself. God spoke to Adam (and Adam understood) on the day mankind was created. On that same day, Adam named the animals, the birds, and the woman created from him. Adam and Eve must have been awesome creatures!

Think for a moment about the complex characteristics required in simply communicating:

- The brain must be wired in such a way that abstractions can be made, language can be learned, and information can be abstracted into the proper code and linguistic structure. In other words, the brain is designed to communicate.
- The human sensory apparatus must be capable of receiving communication and translating it into a form understandable to the brain.
- Information in the brain must somehow be communicated so it can be understood.
- In the case of humans, communication is done through speech, which requires a further set of complex features.[1] These features could not have evolved step by step. They were provided fully formed at the time of creation.

Adam's descendants were pretty awesome also. Within a few generations, humans were living as shepherds, farmers, and cattle herders. Some people lived in cities; others lived as nomads. Some people were constructing and playing musical instruments; others were smelting and forming brass and iron (Genesis 4). Within ten generations, a huge ship or ark was constructed and successfully navigated through the worst storm in earth's history (Genesis 6–8). High culture, complex language, and high intelligence seem to have been present with man from his beginning.

Summary: What Do We Learn about the Artist from What He Has Made?

How does this help our student in evaluating his own involvement in the many "causes" that compete for his attention?

An understanding of man in God's image should give Scott a strong sense of the sanctity of human life. He would know that every human is a special creation of God. Each person on earth—male or female, young or old, unborn or on life support, disabled or not—possesses in full the image of God. As such, every human is to be respected and protected. The image of God given to man by the Creator becomes the foundation for proper treatment of others. It is the proper rationale for developing a Christian ethic in issues as diverse as capital punishment, abortion, and euthanasia.

An understanding of the creation mandate provides a unique foundation for a Christian ethic in environmentalism. The dominion mandate as given by God must not be neglected.

Finally, think about these principles on a personal level. What should it mean to you when you truly understand the implications that God "got His hands dirty" in His creation of you? That God created you in His own image? That God gave you meaningful and important things to do with the life He gave you? That God equipped you physically, mentally, and spiritually in amazing ways to fulfill those responsibilities? These truths should inspire a sense of awe, worship, and confidence.

What's Next?

The following chapter introduces the final division of this book. In part 1, the what, why, how, and when of origins study was presented.

In part 2, we specifically looked at Creation Week and God's creation of the universe, the earth, living things, and finally, mankind. In each area the Artist's work revealed more of the Artist's character and ways. And the more His character and ways were understood, the more we in turn could understand the creation itself. These understandings ultimately help us to see how we are to live our lives in a way that is pleasing to our Creator.

In the remaining chapters we will take Scott, our inquiring student (and you our reader), on a walk through the history of the earth. Just as the Artist reveals Himself in what He has made (part 2), He also reveals Himself in what He has *done*. As we walk through God's workings in history, a framework is formed that will enable our student to understand his culture in the light of biblical truth. As we go, we'll be looking at some fascinating and popular areas of inquiry, such as dinosaurs, fossils, the Flood, the "ice age," and the development of languages and culture.

Consider the Concept

God "got His hands dirty" in order to create mankind. This one act reveals much about God's character and man's worth.

Questions to Ponder

- It all begins with Genesis. Read Genesis 1:26–30; 2:7–8, 15–25. What do you see in these passages that contradicts what is taught by naturalists about man's origins?
- "Made in God's image." What does this mean/not mean? How should this principle affect what you believe and how you live?
- How should a Christian view his responsibility to his environment? Why?

- The following Scriptures teach us much about mankind. As you read the passages, think first about what you are learning about yourself, and second, what you are to do in the light of this knowledge: Job 10:8–9; 33:4–6; Psalm 8:3–7; 39:5; 89:47–48; 100:3; 119:73; 139:13–16; Ecclesiastes 3:10–11.

A Verse to Remember

Yet LORD, You are our Father;
we are the clay, and You are our potter;
we all are the work of Your hands.

Isaiah 64:8

Part 3

Journey through Earth History: What the Artist Has Done

Introduction

In the first and second sections of this book, we looked at beginnings: the beginning of the universe, the earth, living things, and mankind. We examined things both scientific and biblical. Why did we do this? Yes, the study of these things is fascinating. Yes, perplexing questions concerning the Creation/evolution debate are addressed. However, the main reason for the study of origins is to know the Artist—to see more of Him through what He has made and, in turn, to know better how to honor Him as we walk through this life He has given us.

During this the final section of our book, we will walk through biblical earth history, from the time of Creation until God's call on Abraham (Genesis 1–11).

Why this history lesson?

Just as we learn about the Artist from what He has *made,* so we learn about Him from what He has *done.*

A historical framework is vitally important when one desires to truly understand the times in which we live. For example, in order to truly understand the Jewish people in the land of Israel, we must see them in the light of their history—from Father Abraham through the Holocaust and their present struggle to survive as a nation.

How much more important to consider the historical framework of the *entire* human race?

There are several different ideas, or models, of earth history. Each reflects vastly different philosophies of life. One model, naturalism, presents history as beginning 15 to 20 billion years ago. An explosion, in the course of time and through natural processes, led ultimately to the formation of a living cell. This living cell then evolved through time into animals, plants, and humans. Some who hold to this naturalistic model see the process as totally atheistic. The universe and all of time are considered to be random and purposeless. Others attempt to place God, or a "Higher Power," into the mix, resulting in a kind of hybrid mixture of natural plus divine. Others, assuming an Eastern mystical perspective, see a spiritual "god-force" in everything, viewing the history of all things as cyclical, endless repetition.

On the other hand, the biblical model teaches a purposeful Creation by an incredibly intelligent Being Who created with man in mind. The saga of history begins with innocence and continues through a fall into sin and a global, watery judgment on that sinful, violent world. The time frame deals in thousands, not billions, of years.

It is not surprising that, as different as the various versions of earth history are, the resulting philosophies of how life is to be viewed and lived would differ in perhaps even more spectacular form. The question "How shall we then live?" becomes a vital concern.

Our student, Scott, believes in Creation. He has grown up knowing the framework of biblical history. But has he thought through the challenging questions and the details of the implications that this view of history demands? He is about to begin a quest to find out.

We hope you'll join us as we accompany him on this trip.

••

A campus discussion: Is the story of Eden history or Creation myth? Does it matter? The answers have profound implications.

Heidi Howard, Erkel and Associates (Crozet, Va.)

CHAPTER 8
LIFE BEFORE THE FALL: THE EDENIAN EPOCH

ANY college student, indeed almost anyone living in the Western hemisphere, is familiar with the story of Adam and Eve, the serpent, and the Garden of Eden. Of course, the sophisticated academic would not entertain the notion that actual persons or events were involved. Rather, Adam and Eve are usually presented as cartoons, with fig leaves, apples, and snakes whimsically present. It would be considered naïve to believe that there was actually a person, Adam, who lived in an actual place, Eden, and who committed an actual

sin ("What is sin, anyway?") that resulted in death and disease and disaster. It is all prehistoric myth. Besides, how could all this fit in with the naturalistic evolution of mankind? What kind of apelike creature would Adam have been?

Anyway, does it even matter? Does Scott need to believe a Creation myth that will subject him to ridicule by most students and professors? What's the harm in classifying Adam as "just a story"?

The answers are: yes, yes, and plenty! If Adam had not been a real person and the Garden of Eden a real place, and if Adam had not sinned and fallen, then very simply, there would be no need for Christ and the salvation He brings. Sin wouldn't exist. There would be no need for salvation. If Scott negates the historicity of Adam and Eve, the Garden, and the Fall, he might as well eliminate the rest of Scripture as well. Since Scott's faith assures him that this is impossible, he realizes that he needs to know more about the biblical account of Creation.

So let's join Scott as he studies how God the Artist worked in history through these persons and events.

The Garden of Eden

Is it even possible for us to imagine a world without sin? God pronounced His creation "very good" in Genesis 1:31. Now that doesn't mean a grade of B+. The Hebrew word for *good* (*tobe*) means "good in the widest possible sense," and when the word *very* precedes it, the meaning is intensified.

Most of us as children had occasion to pick up a translucent, darkly colored piece of glass. How intriguing it was to look through that glass and see the world around us distorted and colored. Paul may have been referring to something like this when he said in 1 Corinthians 13:12 that "we see indistinctly, as in a mirror" in our present state. Even though what we see now may appear as a beautiful world and interesting people, we are actually looking through distorted glass—there isn't a single person or thing that hasn't been grossly affected by sin.

Genesis 1 and 2 give us the only account of what the world and life in it was like before sin began its reign. We also have descriptions else-where in Scripture of the new creation that will follow the return of Christ, and that too can give us more ideas about what God's perfect original creation may have been like. Let's look at that perfect world and see what we can infer—even if through our dark, warped glasses.

How Long?

The Bible does not tell us how long this period lasted, but it does put some limits on its length. In Genesis 5:3 we are told that Adam had been in existence for 130 years at the birth of his son Seth. Since at his conception Eve considered Seth a replacement for Abel (Genesis 4:25), we know that Seth was conceived after the death of Abel. Since both Abel and his murderer, Cain, were born after Adam and Eve were cast out of the garden (Genesis 4:1–2), the expulsion from the Garden was at least the age of Cain at the slay-ing of his brother subtracted from 130 years. Since maturation rates seem to be a bit longer before the Flood (to be discussed in chap. 12), Cain may have been at least 30 to 60 years old at the time of the murder, putting the upper limit of Adam and Eve's stay in the Garden of Eden at 70 to 100 years.

The fact that Adam and Eve had no children before the Fall poses no restrictions on time. When people live forever, the cen-turies that pass before or between children would mean nothing at all, and it is God's decision when children are born anyway. No bib-lical clues other than these are given on how long the universe remained in this perfect state. Hebrew mythology suggests that the period was seven years, but the number seven may be used in its symbolic sense, not as a measure of actual time.

What Was the World Like before the Fall?

Similarities. In many ways, the world before the Fall was proba-bly similar to the present world. The sky was full of stars; the moon and the sun shone in all their glory. The galaxies we see now were in the sky over Adam's head, as were the planets. Comets were prob-ably in place, as were rings and moons about the planets. The earth had a core, mantle, and crust. The earth had a protective magnetic field and an ozone layer. It had an atmosphere with nitrogen, oxygen, and carbon dioxide needed for the various forms of life. It had dry land and oceans and streams and probably great variety in all. The land and the sea were created with nutrients, with fully developed soils and sediments needed for organisms to live. Water and nutrient cycles were in motion, continually supplying the things needed for the earth's organisms. The heavens and the earth declared the glory of God. They showed His invisible attributes and His character; they provided compelling evidence of their Creator.

Living things on earth during the Edenian Epoch were in some ways very much like they are today. Upon its surface and in its waters and skies, the earth contained a complex array of distinct groups of organisms—from bacteria to protists, algae to fungi, plants to animals. Like every other created thing, they proclaimed the glory of God. The organisms showed beauty and symmetry, order and complexity, variety and unity, mathematical precision and language, abundance and completeness, adaptability and persistence, and provision.

Possible Differences

- *Climate.* Although some young-age creationists have suggested that the world before the Flood lacked rain and climatic seasons, evidence suggests otherwise. Rain is not mentioned in the biblical text before the Flood, but this is probably because rain was too common a phenomenon to mention in such an abbreviated description of earth history. Genesis 1:14 and 8:21–22 suggest that the post-Creation, pre-Flood world did experience seasons. Furthermore, trees preserved in what seem to be Flood sediments indicate that at least some areas of the earth's surface experienced temperate conditions before the Flood. Although there is some evidence in those same trees that the earth might have been a bit warmer than it is today, there is also evidence of wet seasons and dry seasons, even early and late frosts.
- *Land Formations.* The configuration of the continents at

their creation is unknown because the Flood changed their positions substantially. They may have been distributed in the form of the theoretical supercontinent Rodinia. Reconstructions of Rodinia depict the large continents we are familiar with today broken up into pieces and rearranged in orientation and relationship. We don't yet have enough information to determine what the configuration was. One might speculate that the continental pieces made up a group of large islands with extensive, shallow seas between them, cumulatively making up a large region of the tropical to temperate portion of one-half of the southern hemisphere. The remainder of the earth's surface was probably a single, huge ocean.

A very great difference in the Edenian earth was the absence of earthquakes and volcanoes, which seem to be residual effects from the Flood (to be discussed in chap. 12).

- *Oceans.* Were they created salty? We don't know. The identification and study of ocean sediments from the antediluvian world has only begun. Salt crystals have been found in some of these sediments, but more study is needed. Perhaps they were created as fresh water, and the Flood later caused them to become salty.

Since organisms that can only live in salt water today are very common in Flood sediments, some people think the pre-Flood oceans must have been salty as well. But organisms have been created with great potential for change, plus there are species of freshwater organisms that are closely related to species of salt water organisms—possibly part of the same baramin. In addition, some organisms can live in both fresh and saltwater, and some can even migrate between the two.

Those who believe these early oceans were salty point to the salt evidence in the sediments and also to the fact that less biological transformation would be necessary after the Flood. In addition, the sudden mixture of fresh lake waters with salty ocean waters during the Flood may explain the origin of the extensive salt deposits that are seen in Flood sediments.

- *Underground Springs.* Genesis 2:5–6, describing events on Day 6 of Creation Week, tells us that by the time of the creation of man, no rain had fallen upon the dry earth. Genesis 2:6 speaks of a "mist" coming up from the surface of the earth and watering the ground. From this watered ground, God fashioned man, then planted a garden where He would place man. No further reference to this "mist" is made in Scripture. Some have suggested it was a flowing spring (the use of the word in languages similar to Hebrew), a heavy ground fog that dropped a dew, or something else altogether. Indeed, it may have occurred only once in earth history as God prepared the soil right before creating man. We just don't know.

  It is also possible that this word translated "mist" was indeed a spring or flow that may have become the source for the river that came out of Eden and divided into four rivers (Genesis 2:10–14). No other river today divides into four other rivers. (Even though the names Tigris and Euphrates are familiar to us today, they were not the same rivers because they do not come from one river, and the world after the Flood was dramatically different from this original creation.) Considering the extent of the destruction of the Flood (to be discussed in chap. 11), we may never know much more about the pre-Flood rivers than we are told in Genesis 2.

- *The Heavens.* We know there were stars, but we don't know whether stars exploded into supernovas during this period. We know that probably many of the craters on the moon and planets date from the Flood, so we don't know how many craters were there before the Fall. We don't know if asteroids were in existence or if they are the result of a catastrophe at the time of the Flood.

- *Living Creatures.* In spite of the many similarities between organisms living in the Edenian Epoch and those we see today, there were many differences as well. Incredible changes occurred in the baramins following the Flood (see chap. 12). The baramins of the present would probably have existed at the time of Adam and Eve, but many of the particular species with which we are familiar today probably did not. Although elephants were probably named by Adam, neither the Indian nor the African elephant species of today were probably known to him. The same was true of cats and dogs, finches and doves, fruit trees and grasses. Although the animals were similar in general ways, they probably differed from modern species. We might be surprised if we could see a true picture of the animals boarding Noah's ark—the usual picture of giraffes and other common beasts we know today would probably be surprisingly different.[1]

Adam and Eve's Life in the Garden

Genesis 1 and 2 gives us glimpses of what life must have been like in the Garden of Eden. Adam and Eve, before they sinned, were designed to live forever (Genesis 2:17; 3:3). There were no pressures of time commitments; no fevers, sore throats, or viruses to interrupt the routine of life; no pain of arthritis or other problems of aging to contemplate.

We read that they were "naked, yet felt no shame" (Genesis 2:25). This tells us not only something of the climate, but also challenges us to think what life might be like without shame and hiding and fear.

Their diet included only plants—like vegetables and fruit (Genesis 1:29–30). Even the animals ate only plants. The eating of meat entered the world with the Fall. That is a dramatic difference from the world we now know.

How could a world exist without some measure of death? Doesn't eating a carrot kill the carrot plant? The answer to that question seems to be in what Scripture defines as living and dying. In the Bible, life seems to be an attribute only of animals, man, and God. Plants are never described as living or dying. It appears that "life"—as the Bible defines it—is not possessed by individual cells in our bodies or by plants, fungi, algae, protists, or bacteria. And if they are not (biblically) alive, such things cannot (biblically) die. It appears, then, that the entrance of death into the world introduced death for the first time to animals and man. Therefore, the Edenian Epoch not only lacked the natural evils of the eating of flesh, disease, and physical suffering; it also lacked the natural evils of human and animal death. It is likely that pre-Fall animals and humans somehow maintained a state of dynamic equilibrium. When a cell in their bodies ceased to operate, it was promptly replaced through the division of an adjacent cell, thereby maintaining the state of the whole organism indefinitely.

Adam and Eve were busy people, working at cultivating the land and governing the creation they were charged to care for. This work was a happy activity, free from dealing with thorns and thistles and other interfering factors such as harmful insects and droughts. Since animals were not eaten by man or by other animals, there must have been a wonderful relationship with them that was free from fear. We learn in Isaiah 11:6 that someday the lion will lie down with the lamb, and a little child shall also be with them—that indeed must have been the state of the pre-Fall world.

Best of all, Adam and Eve enjoyed a continuous relationship with their Creator. It is presumed (from Genesis 3:8) that the couple regularly walked and talked with God. No fear, no sin, and daily beholding His love, His care, and His glory—this is difficult for those of us who view the Word through the distorted, dark glasses of the post-Fall world to even imagine.

Summary: What We Learn about the Artist from What He Has Done

- The Artist is a "very good" God Who hates sin, violence, and death. He created a "very good" world—free from death and suffering. Only the young-age interpretation of earth history presents a world where death, suffering, and struggle for survival were ever absent. Even old-age creationist models affirm that death of animals, disease, and suffering had to have been a permanent part of the created order. The Bible teaches a time to come when there will be a perfect "new heavens and earth," where sin and suffering is no more. We are much more able to grasp this promise in its fullness when we recognize that God's *original* creation was "very good" in the same sense. When we lose the sense of something better beyond our present experience, we are apt to slip into a dark pit of discouragement and depression. Hope is the result of knowing the God Who cared enough to create in such a fashion (and to redeem the fallen creature through Jesus—but that story is still to come).

- The Artist is a God of abundance. He provided abundantly, excessively, not merely the necessities of life but so much more.
- The Artist is Sovereign, Providential. He created the perfect world knowing that it would be marred by sin and would need to survive in order for God's sovereign plan through His Son to be completed.

What's Next?

Earth history begins with God's idea of the best for us. Only by having a good understanding of the Edenian Epoch can we adequately grasp the extent and tragedy of the turn that was taken when man disobeyed. We'll focus on this time in the chapter that follows.

Consider the Concept

God created a world that was "very good" and very different from the present world we know. It was a time when death and sin did not exist.

Questions to Ponder

- Why is it important to affirm that Adam and Eve were actual historical people? How would this concept conflict with the teaching in a modern anthropology class?
- When we contemplate the earth at the end of Creation Week, we seem to have more questions than answers about land masses, oceans, climate, and even what the creatures looked like. The later judgments of the Fall and the Flood have masked our view of the original creation. As you read through the section of the chapter that discussed these things, summarize what *may* have been different and why. Is there anything we *know* to be different?
- Describe "a day in the life of Adam and Eve." Use your informed imagination. What did they eat? What did they wear? How did they spend their time?
- Did death of animals exist before the Fall? How could a world exist without death in some form? How does the Bible define *living?*
- When we look at God's description of what His perfect "new heavens and earth" will be like, we can see parallels with the original created order. Read Isaiah 11:6–9 and Revelation 21:9–22:5 and note the parallels you see.
- Is there anything in this chapter that surprised you? Got your attention? Made you want to learn more? What questions did this chapter provoke in your thinking?

A Verse to Remember

God saw all that He had made, and it was very good. Evening came, and then morning: the sixth day.

Genesis 1:31

CHAPTER 9
THE FALL

WHATEVER happened to sin?

Sin is not a popular word at the beginning of the twenty-first century—and *definitely* not on the campus of a modern university. The widespread involvement in alcohol abuse, drugs, and sexual promiscuity among students may be called "not cool" or "a result of poor choices," but never sin. The postmodern idea that "anything goes" certainly trumps old-fashioned moral, biblical absolutes.

In the midst of all the decadent ideas and lifestyles, God has spoken through what He has done—some six thousand years ago in the Garden—in bringing judgment upon man's clear disobedience and in clearly showing that it isn't a "mistake" or a "poor choice" or the consequences of poverty and societal ills—it is *sin*.

Does sin really matter? Isn't it merely a matter of personal responsibility, in which an individual must deal with the consequences of his "poor choices"?

When Adam and Eve believed Satan's lie, "you will be like God" (Genesis 3:5), and chose to disobey God, they plunged the entire cosmos into a state like nothing they could have imagined.

In a matter of moments, sin entered the world and with it, death. Immediately, spiritual death—separation from God—became a reality, and the changes necessary for physical death began as well.

In a matter of moments, fear and shame entered the couple's consciousnesses, and relationships were shattered. Blame shifting occurred as Adam not only blamed Eve for his sin but also blamed

God for giving Eve to him. Both Adam and Eve hid from God. Within a generation, violence and murder would also become reality.

In a matter of moments, changes also began in the physical universe. No other event in the history of the physical universe has been so dramatic. It's likely that the sum of all the changes that have occurred since that monumental event does not begin to approach the magnitude of the drastic change recorded in Genesis 3. The world as Adam and Eve knew it took on a darker feel as a new epoch in earth history began.

Yes, sin matters.

Why the Fall?

What brought about this change in the created order? *Sin.* The curse was specifically a response to the sin of man. And notice that it was a response to their sin, not a direct result of it. After Adam and Eve sinned, their perception was immediately changed, but it does not seem that the world around them changed at the same instant. After their sin, humans could apparently still live forever (by eating of the tree of life: Genesis 3:22–24). It was not the sin of man that caused the world to change; it was God's *response* to the sin of man—in the form of the curse.

Death and Decay in the Universe: The Law of the Fall

Scripture suggests that this curse was applied to the entire universe. We read in Psalm 102:25–26: "Long ago You established the earth, and the heavens are the work of Your hands. They will perish, but You will endure; all of them will wear out like clothing. You will change them like a garment, and they will pass away." Romans 8:20–22 also speaks of this curse: "For the creation was subjected to futility—not willingly, but because of Him who subjected it—in the hope that the creation itself will also be set free from the bondage of corruption into the glorious freedom of God's children. For we know that the whole creation has been groaning together with labor pains until now."

God did something in response to the Fall of man to cause the entire universe to age, to deteriorate.

Perhaps this change was accomplished by the suspension of one law from the original creation—a law that restored heat energy *from* the universe to energy generators *in* the universe. With such a law (or one similar to it) still in effect, the energy of the universe would be constantly cycled and never run out. Without such a law, heat energy would be unusable and would accumulate in the universe. This is due to another natural law we know today as the Second Law of Thermodynamics (discussed in chap. 4). The Second Law maintains that the energy of the universe tends to move toward a state of entropy or disorder. Energy tends to move from a carefully packaged form (such as in stars and molecules) to a spread-out, unpackaged form (like dissipated heat energy). A consequence of the Second Law is that complex systems tend to break down. Systems—even the universe as a whole—tend to age, deteriorate, and depart steadily further from their initial design.

The largest-scale features of the curse seem to be generated by this Second Law of Thermodynamics. Yet the Second Law predated the curse; this same principle that deteriorates large-scale complexity also causes oxygen to pass into the blood from the air, and it causes carbon dioxide to enter the air from the blood. It causes digestive juices to spread through the food in the intestine and provides for necessary food molecules to be taken into the blood and then into body cells. It drives waste products from the blood, and it drives life-enhancing water into the tissues.

So it appears that what caused the large-scale effects of the curse may not have been the introduction of a *new* law (the Second Law of Thermodynamics) but the suspension of some other law. It is interesting that something designed for good (the Second Law) in the original creation could—with as "small" a change as the suspension of another law—cause what is generally perceived as huge negative effects.

There is at least one more interesting side effect from the Second Law as we know it today. According to this law, there is a tendency for complex systems (including the universe) to change downward (or devolve) in complexity, rather than to change upward (or evolve) in complexity. It seems strange indeed that traditional evolutionary theory requires systems to increase in complexity. Somehow, the Second Law has to be overcome for this (the evolution of the universe or the evolution of life) to take place.

If you recall from chapter 4, the Second Law, in order to be overcome, seems to require three things: (1) an external energy source, (2) an energy converter, and (3) some sort of plan for organizing the energy. If God does not exist, all three of these things are missing from the evolution of the universe. If God does exist but does not intervene in the evolution of life, all but the energy source is missing. Although the Second Law fits into a creationist understanding of the universe's history, it seems to stand as a significant barrier to nontheistic histories.

Biological Effects of the Fall

Many problems we face today in our world were introduced as sin and death began their reign following the Fall.

- *Mutations and Disease.* One effect of the Fall was the lessening of efficiency in biological systems. Before the Fall, genetic information was apparently copied without error. The mechanism by which this occurred is unknown, but for biological systems to persist indefinitely, errorless copying seems to be essential. Beginning after the Fall, genetic copying errors (mutations) entered the world and began to accumulate in the DNA of organisms. Some mutations compromised the design of the organism, leading to failed or impaired function. This led to diseases such as diabetes and sickle-cell anemia.

    Some mutations caused entire populations of organisms to change their behavior and begin to hurt other organisms. Examples are parasites and pathological bacteria. In the young-age creationist model, these diseases are the result of small imperfections in otherwise magnifi-

cently designed systems. This would explain how two similar strains of the Ebola virus could impact humans in
such radically different ways—one not harmful at all; the
other, one of the deadliest disease organisms known to
man. Young-age creationism suggests that mutations are a
recent, rather than an old, feature of life. The low mutational load of organisms (see chap. 6) seems to confirm
this expectation.

- *Overproduction.* Before the time of the Fall, organisms were
  supposed to reproduce until they filled the earth. It is
  likely that once this happened, the generation of young
  would cease. This in turn suggests that God fashioned
  organisms with efficient reproductive mechanisms that
  produced only as many offspring as needed, expecting all
  of them to survive. Unless this changed at the Fall, disease
  and death would gradually (or perhaps quickly) wipe out
  organisms on the earth. To counter this, God apparently
  introduced overproduction into the biological world.
  Since many organisms would die before they reproduced,
  more offspring had to be produced than would survive.
  This explains the extra work that man had to do after the
  Fall to get rid of certain plants (weeds) that were overpro-
  ducing and competing with the desired food crops
  (Genesis 3:18–19).
- *Natural Selection.* God created organisms to survive not
  just before the Fall but through changes in the earth that
  He knew would follow after the Fall. This shows that He
  created a great capacity in organisms to change and to
  pass those changes on to the next generation. This heredi-
  tary variation combined with overproduction creates what
  is commonly known as "natural selection." Organisms
  were forced to struggle against other organisms for limited
  resources. Those that were able to adapt to changes in
  those resources or to specialize on different resources
  tended to survive. Natural selection in young-age creation

theory is a process created by God to maintain His creatures through changes on the earth that followed the Fall.

- *Thorns.* With the introduction of disease and the overgrazing that came as a result of overproduction, the plants became prone to extinction unless they were protected. God apparently provided thorns and tannins to accomplish this task. This explains why thistles and thorns came after the Fall (Genesis 3:18).

- *Carnivory.* Animals were also at risk of being wiped out by disease unless some mechanism was introduced to protect them. The eating of flesh, or carnivory, seems to fulfill that function. Since carnivores tend to eat the slower prey, diseased and young organisms are the ones most often eaten. This increases the fitness of the entire population. As awful as animals eating other animals seems to be, it is providential in a world where disease reigns.

Exactly when all these changes occurred is not clear. Whether organisms were transformed immediately or whether they produced these changes in the years, decades, or centuries after the Fall is not clarified in Scripture. Based upon the fossils found in what we interpret to be Flood sediments, we infer that carnivory and disease had become widespread by the time of Noah's Flood.

The young-age creation model suggests that these biological evils of death, disease, struggle for survival, poisons, thorns, and carnivory were all a consequence of man's sin. Other theistic models of origins are forced by their time lines to claim that all these things preceded man's sin and are part of the world the way God created it. Since this seems to strain the conventional understanding of goodness and mercy, the young-age creation model for the origin of biological natural evil is more consistent with the nature of God as revealed in Scripture.[1]

Human Life "East of Eden"

Adam and Eve were evicted from the Garden—"east of Eden," the Scriptures tell us (Genesis 3:24). No more walking with God in the cool of the evening, no more "free lunches" at the tree of life and other fruitful trees, no more enjoying the benefits of being vice-regents in charge of a nonrebellious earth. From that time forward, it would all be *work*.

Life changed in many ways. A few are mentioned here:

- *Toil and Labor.* Man had been given a dominion mandate—to care for and nurture God's creation. Rather than the joyful experience it had been before, caring for the creation became a daunting task—simply to survive. Before the Fall, the tasks man had were probably rewarded with enjoyment similar to the refreshment we receive in participating in our favorite hobbies. After the Fall, it would take great effort to carve out a living.

- *Man vs. Animals.* Before the Fall, animals did not die. After the Fall, animals would not only die, but man would be forced to kill them in order to atone for his sin. After the Flood, animals would be given an innate fear of man, and man could kill them for food. The ravages of disease, the failures in the struggle for survival, the attacks of animals upon man, and the animals being eaten by other animals would be agonizing, continual reminders of the consequences of human sin and the inadequacy of man to fulfill the dominion mandate.

- *Human Suffering.* Much more pain would be involved in the activities of life, like child-bearing (Genesis 3:16)—a kind of pain exceeding that which is necessary to alert us to danger, such as when pain tells us to take our hand off the stove to keep from being burned. This new level of pain and suffering—death, disease, human abuse—would cause emotional, physical, and spiritual suffering that never existed before the Fall.

- *Shame.* According to Scripture, Adam and Eve were naked before the Fall (Genesis 2:25), with nothing to hide. As soon as they sinned, they became ashamed of their nakedness, apparently because it represented their sinful condition. They made clothes from fig leaves and hid themselves from God (Genesis 3:7–8). After God pronounced the curse, He killed an animal to make clothes for Adam and Eve (Genesis 3:21).

In this death—perhaps the first death ever to occur on earth—God graphically showed man the consequences of his sin. Imagine the horror that Adam and Eve must have felt at seeing the death of an innocent animal, impressing upon them the magnitude of their sin. It was a first glimpse of what they had done and of what would have to be done to redeem them. Fig leaves were not to be a proper covering since blood would have to be shed for their sin. It would require the death of a living being.

A Case Study: Evolutionary Theory— Natural Selection and Mutation

Biology 101. The terms *natural selection* and *mutation* appear in virtually all high school and college textbooks as the mechanism used by evolution to bring all the various groups of living things into being. Natural selection and mutation are the "bread and butter" of the theory. Let's once more put principle into practice and examine the claim in the light of biblical principles, observation of the data, and interpretation that is consistent with Scripture's claims.

Natural selection has been defined as the preferential survival of those individuals who have inherited characteristics that give them an advantage in the environment in which they find themselves. ("Survival of the fittest" is the popularized term.) Charles Darwin introduced this theory in 1859. In bioevolutionary theory, natural selection is thought to have been a part of life from its very beginning—more than four billion years ago. Natural selection is thought to be how advantageous changes are chosen over other changes and thus, ultimately, how organisms have changed through time.

Mutations are errors made when cells copy DNA—usually the loss, insertion, or change of a nucleotide in a DNA molecule. Bioevolutionary theory also claims mutation to have been a part of life from its very beginning. Mutations are credited to be the major source of the genetic change needed for organisms to evolve their way through the "tree of life."

Consistent with Biblical Truth?

The first question the inquiring biology student must ask is "Is this theory consistent with biblical truth?" Even a quick read of the Book of Genesis would reveal a conflict. Biblical claims involve the creation of created "kinds," denying the single-ancestor proposal. The time frame of these evolutionary principles also is in direct conflict with the claims of Scripture. Even more of a conflict is the challenge to the character of God—could He have created life through a process of struggle, violence, and death?

Examine the Data: Is There Another Way of Looking at It?

In young-age creation theory, natural selection was a process God introduced following man's Fall about six thousand years ago. Natural selection is a natural consequence of two things: variety of inherited characteristics and overpopulation. In Creation Week, God established heritable variety in organisms to perpetuate the variety that reflects His nature. With the Fall of man, the entrance of mutation, death, and disease would have destroyed that variety unless something was introduced to maintain it. God apparently did that at the Fall by introducing "overproduction" (organisms producing more offspring that would survive long enough to create offspring of their own). The resulting natural selection functions to preserve the variety of organisms in the face of mechanisms that tend to destroy them.

In carefully studied cases (e.g., the famous peppered moth) natural selection (1) involves rather small changes, (2) usually dampens change (e.g., the increase in numbers of dark peppered moths during the second half of the nineteenth century was reversed during the first half of the twentieth century), and (3) works most effectively in taking out harmful mutations. Natural selection seems to act more to prevent organisms from changing (as suggested in young-age creation theory) rather than facilitating their change (as suggested in evolutionary theory).

Mutation is also thought to have begun only after man's Fall. Given that organisms were created optimally, mutation is thought to have gradually degenerated the perfect genetic information God created in organisms during the Creation Week. Mutation is probably responsible for much of the pathology (disease) of the world.

Of carefully studied mutations, most have been found to be harmful to organisms, and most of the remainder seem to have neither positive nor negative effect. Mutations that are actually beneficial are extraordinarily rare and involve insignificant changes. Mutations seem to be much more degenerative than constructive, just as young-age creation theory would suggest. Additionally, the number of mutations in organisms seems closer to the number that might be generated in thousands rather than billions of years of life history.

Summary: What We Learn about the Artist from What He Has Done

Life's lessons teach us more of the character of God. We need to ask, "What do we learn about our God from the events surrounding the Fall of man?"

Obviously, we see a *God Who is Holy.* He can't look at sin. He can't grade "on a curve." He is also a *God of justice:* He keeps His promises, responding to man's disobedience as He said He would.

But perhaps even more overwhelmingly, we see a *God of mercy.* The Creator knew, long before man sinned, that man *would* sin. Before the foundation of the world, God had provided redemption, through the work of His Son.

Even before God pronounced the curse on the man, He gave the first hint of the salvation that was to come. He said to the serpent, "He [the seed of the woman] will strike your head, and you will strike his heel" (Genesis 3:15). Theologians interpret this passage as a prophecy of the battle between the evil one and mankind, a battle in which he ultimately will be crushed. "Striking his heel" is most likely a reference to the future crucifixion of Jesus, the Seed of the woman. While this passage seems obscure to us, it evidently was not obscure to Adam and Eve, who took hope from God's pronouncement.

What amazing mercy and love this God possesses! Instead of squashing the disobedient creatures (as you or I would probably have done had we been God), He optimized the conditions of the fallen world in such a way that mankind would survive and ultimately have a way back to Him. The devastation was not as bad as it could have been.

Consider the following examples:

- When Adam and Eve tried to cover themselves with fig leaves, God provided them with clothing made from skins instead. This first blood sacrifice established a way for man to come to Him and to make atonement for their sins (Genesis 3:21).

- God sent Adam and Eve from the Garden in order to prevent them from eating from the tree of life (Genesis 3:22–24). The tree of life would have allowed them to live forever physically while still being dead spiritually. God did not wish them to live in eternal separation from Him. He had a better plan.

- Biological changes that indeed seem bad—such as mutations, overpopulation, carnivory, and thorns—actually served a preserving, protecting function in enabling the creation to survive in a fallen world. God had created organisms to survive not just before the Fall but through changes in the earth that He knew would follow after the Fall.

What's Next?

Now cursed, the creation entered a new era. In many ways it was an era much like today's, but the great reworking of the earth that would be accomplished by the Flood had not yet occurred. Some highlights of this post-Edenian Epoch of earth history, called the Antediluvian (before the Flood) Epoch, will be summarized in the next chapter.

Consider the Concept

One who interprets the rocks and fossils of the earth's crust as representing billions of years of earth history must also agree that death, disease, poisons, and struggle for survival were a part of the natural order long before man appeared on the scene.

Questions to Ponder

- How often do you hear the word *sin* spoken on a college campus? Discuss why this biblical concept is so unpopular today.
- God did something in response to the Fall of man to cause the entire universe to age, to deteriorate. Did you understand the discussion in this chapter about the Second Law of Thermodynamics? Please read it again and then prepare an explanation that you could present to your physics professor.
- In your own words, define *mutation* and *natural selection*. How do these fit into young-earth creation theory? How does evolutionary theory differ in its use of these terms?
- Describe a day in the life of Adam and Eve *after* the Fall.
- What do we learn of God's holiness, mercy, and love from the events of Genesis 3?
- Is there anything in this chapter that surprised you? Got your attention? Made you want to learn more? What questions did this chapter provoke in your thinking?

A Verse to Remember

For the creation was subjected to futility—not willingly, but because of Him who subjected it—in the hope that the creation itself will also be set free from the bondage of corruption into the glorious freedom of God's children. For we know that the whole creation has been groaning together with labor pains until now.

Romans 8:20–22

CHAPTER 10
LIFE BEFORE THE FLOOD: THE ANTEDILUVIAN WORLD

THE portion of earth history we are about to describe in this chapter would seem so far-fetched to most academic minds that Scott would probably be laughed off campus. Virtually *everything* described in Genesis 4–6 would be denied: people who lived an average of nine hundred years? people who built cities, forged iron and bronze, and crafted musical instruments—all in the first generations after Adam? In conventional thinking, primitive man could never have accomplished those things. Furthermore, the likelihood that a man named Noah really lived and built a big boat that floated through a worldwide deluge with a bunch of animals on board would be rejected instantly. This period would be a hard sell to our twenty-first-century culture.

However, the pre-Flood time in history is important to those who hold a biblical worldview. The curse begins to be played out in time as the phrase "and he died" is repeated over and over. And throughout this period we once more see the character of the Artist Who reveals Himself by what He does.

Let's talk about it.

What would it have been like to live between the Fall and the Flood? This intriguing time in earth history, covering a period of approximately 1,600 years, is recorded only in Genesis 4–6. Other hints of what the world was like during this time can be gleaned from studying the evidence from the fossil record of the Flood. In this chapter we'll stretch our thinking a bit to visualize a time that was in many ways similar to our own, but in other ways much different.

Life for Adam and His Kin

At first glance, reading the genealogies of Scripture seems boring and tedious—perhaps something to skip over to get to the "good stuff" more quickly. However, the record of the descendants of Adam to Noah found in Genesis 4 and 5 gives us a wealth of information about this period of history. Some of the key observations are briefly noted below.

- *Death reigned.* An obvious repeated phrase in the passage was "and he died." Life in the fallen world had become a reality (Genesis 5).

- *Man had advanced culture from the beginning.* We read accounts of life during this period that include farming, shepherding, the building of cities, musical instruments, brass and iron workers, and the building of a large barge (Genesis 4–6).

- *Sin and violence increased.* Beginning with Cain's murder of Abel, the record continues with Lamach, who killed two men who merely hurt his feelings (Genesis 4:23) and then bragged about it. By Genesis 6, "the earth was corrupt in God's sight, and the earth was filled with violence" (v. 11), and "the LORD saw that man's wickedness was widespread on the earth and that every scheme his mind thought of was nothing but evil all the time" (v. 5).

- *There was a godly/righteous remnant.* Genesis 4:26 tells us that during Seth's lifetime, people began to worship the Lord. We know that God had already provided a sacrificial system that was in place when Cain and Abel brought their offerings to the Lord. We also hear of two men in the line of Seth who were clearly called "righteous." Enoch (Genesis 5:21–24) "walked with God" and had the unique privilege of being taken to heaven by God without dying. Noah also was called "a righteous man" (Genesis 6:9). It was through the line of Seth to Noah that the Savior would one day come.

- *Humans could marry their siblings.* It was possible for Cain to marry one of his sisters without negative genetic consequences. At this point, organisms carried a low mutational load.

- *Humans lived a long time.* The average lifespan of Adam through Noah (except Enoch, who did not die) was 912 years. After the Flood, the generation time drops from the 950 years that Noah lived to the 205 years that the father of Abraham lived.

How can this be? Much speculation about this question has occurred. Although it has been suggested by many that the change in life spans was due to environment, it is more likely that the change was genetic. Several observations lead to this conclusion.

First, experimentation on animals has been unable to increase the maximum death age of organisms by changing their environment.

Second, the change in human life span documented in Scripture occurred over a long period of time. In fact, Moses' generation was still living consistently for 120 years approximately one thousand years after the Flood. Although temperature and rainfall changed during this period, none of the changes that are thought to have occurred seem capable of changing human longevity.

A *third* consideration is that although aging is not fully understood, it appears that it is genetically controlled. Early in development, cells in our bodies divide to take the place of adjacent cells that die. If this function were never turned off, it is likely that human organs could be maintained much longer than they are. But most cell types in the body quit replacing adjacent cells at some point. After this, tissue degenerates. Different tissues have different moments when replacement actually stops, and the body ages as more and more tissues deteriorate in this manner. The life span of the human body, then, is programmed in the genetics of the cells.

It is likely that a different programming existed in the antediluvian world.

A Description of the Pre-Flood World

For most of the information we have about the antediluvian world, we must lean on inferences from the evidence that remains—largely the evidence left in the fossil record of the Flood. This is a new area of research for young-age creationism, and it is likely that the ideas expressed here will be modified as more work is done. In the remainder of this chapter we will present several intriguing and interesting ideas about the world Adam and his kin may have experienced.

The Floating Forest: A Beautiful, but Different, World

The God Who loves diversity seems to have created organisms in a fascinating array of unique communities—communities that were destroyed in the Flood. After the Flood, land animals and much of their food had to disperse from the same location. This means that the different communities we know today developed from similar stock, so the differences among present communities are probably much less than the differences originally created in antediluvian communities.

For example, more than 88 percent of the plant species in the present world are classified in one division (or phylum) of plants—*Anthophyta*, or flowering plants. If we are properly identifying the rocks that were formed in post-Flood times, it seems that flowering plants have been the dominant plant on earth since the Flood. But that may not have been the case *before* the Flood—at least not everywhere on earth.

The lowest great division of Flood rocks was originally called the Primary. Although the Primary rocks contain many plant fossils (most of the world's coal, for example), they contain no flowering plants at all. Instead, the plants are from divisions that are either extinct or are represented in today's world by relatively few species. Actually, most of the fossils of the Primary—including sediments closely associated with those containing plants—were not plants at all but sea creatures. Even most of the world's coal (which is formed from a dense accumulation of plant material) is surrounded and even invaded by sediments containing fossils of sea creatures. It is almost as if the plants of the Primary were somehow associated with the animals of the ocean. (For a further explanation of Primary rocks, see "A Case Study" on p. 129, as well as the illustration on p. 132.)

Based upon these findings, it has been proposed that the Primary plants actually formed the basis of a large floating forest biome[1] (a *biome* is a major ecological community type, such as rain forest, desert, etc.). Based upon how much organic material made up the coals of the Primary, this floating forest may have been sub-continent-sized or even continent-sized.

The basic structure was probably broadly similar to the "quaking bogs" found on a number of lakes in the upper Midwestern United States. Quaking bogs are floating vegetation mats whose outer edges are made up of aquatic plants. These aquatic plants expand the edge of the mat by means of rootlike extensions known as *rhizomes*. Farther in from the edge of the mat, where plants have been growing for some time, the intertwined rhizomes are dense enough to capture a bit of soil in which small land plants can grow. Even farther in, where the mat is thicker and has been there longer, enough soil accumulates for larger plants to grow. This pattern continues as the distance from the open water increases, until a soil layer thick enough to support full-sized trees and all the understory plants of an entire forest is developed. These floating plants also provide a home for animals.

A similar ecosystem is proposed for the floating forest biome of the antediluvian world.

Since the choppy seas of the Flood probably destroyed the floating forest from the outside in, the plants on the edge of the floating
forest were probably the lowermost plants of the Primary. The
plants just inside the edge of the floating forest were probably
buried next, and so on.

If indeed such forests existed in the pre-Flood world, they
would explain a number of features observed in the fossil record of
the Primary:

   1. The floating forest biome was not likely to re-form in
   the choppy seas following the Flood. This would explain why
   most of the "land" plants and "land" animals of the Primary
   are extinct today.

   2. The plants from the edge to the center of such a floating
   forest would progress from plants that loved water and needed
   it to survive to plants that needed less water. The series of
   divisions of plants in the Primary shows just such a progression—from those plants that require standing water for reproduction to those that need less and less standing water.

   3. The plants in the Primary from the bottom up show a
   progression from short to tall—just as is true in quaking bogs
   today.

   4. Most of the plants in the Primary do not have true
   roots. They have rhizomes instead—rootlike structures that
   seem to be incapable of penetrating true soils. But they would

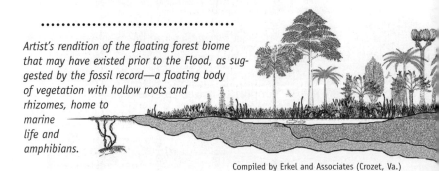

*Artist's rendition of the floating forest biome
that may have existed prior to the Flood, as suggested by the fossil record—a floating body
of vegetation with hollow roots and
rhizomes, home to
marine
life and
amphibians.*

Compiled by Erkel and Associates (Crozet, Va.)

be capable of intertwining with rhizomes of other plants to create a floating forest.

5. Many of the plants of the Primary—especially the large ones—are hollow. Very often their rhizomes, their branches, and even their main trunks contain large cavities, as if the entire plant was designed to weigh less for the purpose of floating.

6. The most common rhizome in the coal plants, *Stigmaria,* is hollow, circular in cross-section, and large in diameter. Departing at right angles to the surface of this rhizome in every direction around it are small, hollow rootlets. Neither the rhizomes nor the rootlets seem to be designed to penetrate soils, but they are similar to the smaller-scale root-like structures of several plants that float in water.

7. Among the animals preserved in the Primary sediments are large amphibians that look like intermediates between fish and land animals. Such animals would seem to be designed to live in the pools of water that might be scattered along the floor of such a floating forest—in the ecologically intermediate position between sea and land that such pools would afford.

Dinosaurs

Everyone wants to know about dinosaurs. How do these creatures, claimed to have existed 65 million years ago, fit into the biblical picture? Since dinosaurs are known to us from sediments we
believe to have been deposited in the Flood, they must have lived
in the pre-Flood world. Since the dinosaurs are land animals, they
must have been created on Day 6 of Creation Week and lived on the
earth at the same time as man in the pre-Flood world. They also, as
land animals, would have been part of the population that boarded
the ark.

But probably Adam and his descendants didn't have a whole lot
of contact with these interesting beasts. The reasons for this conclusion are also found in observations from the fossil record.

In the same layers with the dinosaurs are found animals and
plants that we either don't see at all on the earth today or see only
infrequently. There are animals found with dinosaurs that are classified as mammals (based upon their teeth) but are strange mammals. With the possible exception of the opossum, no modern
mammal group is found with the dinosaurs.

As for plants, flowering plants tend to be found only rarely with
the dinosaurs. Instead, the dinosaurs are generally found with gymnospermous plants—the "naked-seed" plants that do not have
flowers. In the present world, the naked-seed plants (like cycads and
ginkgos) appear to be rarer than they were in association with the
dinosaurs. This suggests that the dinosaurs probably ate gymnosperms. Since they ate different foods, it is likely that dinosaurs
lived in a separate location from humans. In fact, the gymnosperms
probably formed the foundation of a separate biome than the one
in which humans lived. Perhaps one or more island continents
housed the gymnosperm/dinosaur biome, while other island continents housed the angiosperm/mammal/man biome.

It is also likely that the gymnosperm/dinosaur biome
was located at a lower altitude or closer to the shore of the
antediluvian world. This would explain why members of the

In pre-Flood times, as suggested by the fossil record, dinosaurs probably lived separated from man, in a biome dominated by gymnospermous plants.

Erkel and Associates (Crozet, Va.)

gymnosperm/dinosaur biome are consistently buried beneath members of the other biome. This is also consistent with the biblical claim (inferred from Eden's river that branched into four rivers) that the Garden of Eden was a high point geographically.

Stromatolite Forests

A strange and different picture of the world seems to be emerging as we try to visualize the pre-Flood earth. In addition to areas that featured floating forests with their amphibians and others that housed dinosaurs and their gymnosperm plants, we find yet another unique biome of the antediluvian world—that of stromatolites. Stromatolites are dome-shaped structures made up of layers upon layers of organic material alternating with some sort of sediment such as sand. The organic layers of modern stromatolites are made from communities of bacteria and are rare and relatively small in the present world. They tend to grow in extreme environments, such as hot springs or salty bays. These bacterial communities provide desirable food for a variety of animals.

In the fossil record, stromatolites tend to be relatively common, at least in what seem to be antediluvian sediments. They tend to present a lot of evidence of hot spring activity and seem to be located near the margins of pre-Flood continents. It may be that offshore, around some of the antediluvian continents, God created a long, wide zone of hot springs that generated ideal living conditions for algae and bacteria to produce extensive stromatolite reefs. These hot springs may have been more of the "fountains of the great deep" that were broken up at the beginning of the Flood. Perhaps this catastrophic breakup is why such stromatolite reefs no longer exist in the present.

Like coral reefs of today, the offshore stromatolite reefs may have protected a lagoon between the reefs and the shoreline from severe storms. In these lagoons—perhaps especially in the warm waters closer to the reefs—the strange animals we see preserved in the lowermost Flood strata may have lived.

The fossil record suggests the possibility of the pre-Flood existence of a stromato-lite biome—offshore reefs that protected the shoreline and fostered some of the now extinct animals who enjoyed the warm and wet conditions.

Erkel and Associates (Crozet, Va.)

A Case Study: The "Geologic Column"

Any student of life or earth sciences encounters, early in his career, some sort of diagram that seeks to explain the rock layers (also called "strata") of the earth. The Geologic Column (the Rock, or Stratigraphic, Column plus geologic time) was first devised in the nineteenth century as the science of geology was developing. Even casual observers are able to note the fascinating rocks, which had been deposited with their fossils like a huge multilayered cake upon the basement rocks of planet earth. These sediments cover much of the earth's surface. They reach a thickness of sixty thousand feet in some areas, averaging a thickness of more than one mile on the planet.

Today, in virtually every high school and university setting, the *interpretation* of these sedimentary rocks sounds something like this:

1. The lowest layers of rock, called "Precambrian," represent sediments deposited approximately 3,800 to 530 million
years ago. During this vast eon of time, bacteria evolved into

algae and protists, and fossils include stromatolites and tiny microorganisms.

2. The layers that rest on top of the "Precambrian" are called "Paleozoic." These Paleozoic (formerly called "Primary") strata represent sediments deposited approximately 530 to 248 million years ago. During this era of time, microorganisms evolved into animals and plants of both the sea and the land, and fossils in these strata include many marine organisms, plants, and amphibians.

3. The next layers in the upward progression of strata are called "Mesozoic" (or "Secondary"), believed to have been deposited 248 to 65 million years in the past. These strata are said to represent "middle life" and include the famous dinosaurs and other reptiles.

4. The uppermost layers, with dates assigned from 65 million years to the present, are termed "Tertiary" and "Quaternary," with the Quaternary being the most recent epoch of 2 million years. The Tertiary and Quaternary together are dubbed the "Cenozoic," which means "recent life," said to record the evolution of mammals and, most recently, man.

Consistent with Biblical Truth?

Our student, Scott's, first question should be "Is this interpretation consistent with the clear teachings of Scripture?" The answer is, of course, "No." The biblical timeline in no way accommodates "eons," "eras," "periods," or "epochs" that provide time gaps of many millions of years between the creation of sea-dwelling creatures and man. The Bible also teaches the concept of "created kinds," not macroevolution. The Bible further speaks of a worldwide flood, whose record should be easily found in the record of the earth's sediments.

Examine the Data: Is There Another Way of Looking at It?

The actual rock and fossil record does not come with dates attached to it—the extended lengths of time are clearly the result of nonbiblical assumptions. How then does the young-age creationist geologist interpret this data?

Clearly, the rocks reveal something about the past. But what? Instead of millions of years of evolutionary development, the Bible speaks of periods of history such as pre-Flood, Flood, and post-Flood.

Because a global flood would involve the deposit of *huge* amounts of sediment, it is believed that a large portion of the rock record is indeed a record of the Flood and the tumultuous centuries following the Flood. The record of the many creatures entombed in those rocks does not indicate an evolution of life throughout the ages, but rather present a snapshot of living things at that particular event in earth history.

In this chapter, the understanding of the pre-Flood world with its possible biomes of floating forests, gymnosperms, and stromatolites was discussed. The interpretation was based upon a study of the Precambrian and Primary rocks of the Stratigraphic Column. As we study the Flood and post-Flood period in the coming chapters of this book, the interpretation of the Flood and post-Flood rocks will be discussed. Although creationists today are still working through exactly where Flood and post-Flood boundaries are found in the rock record, the authors of this book currently interpret the Primary and Secondary rocks as Flood sediments and the Tertiary/Quaternary rocks as post-Flood. (Note: for clarification see the illustration on the next page.) We will not use the terms *Paleozoic, Mesozoic,* and *Cenozoic* because they imply eras of time and evolutionary development.

Summary: What We Learn about the Artist from What He Has Done

The Artist's *love of diversity* is evident in the wide range of plants and animals that flourished in the floating forests and other biomes of the pre-Flood world.

We also note God's *patience* during a time of increasing sin and violence. His love for those He created caused Him to wait and warn before bringing the promised destruction upon the earth.

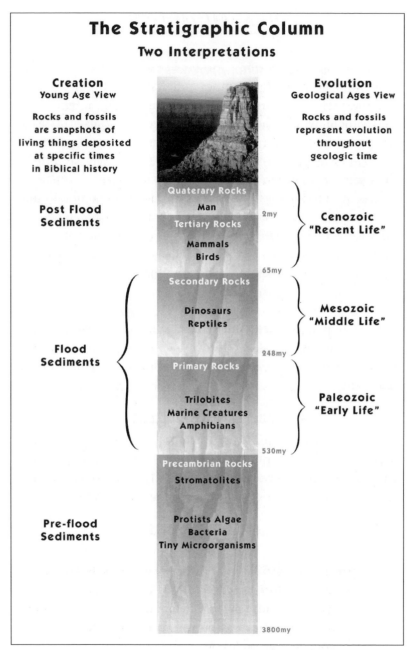

The Stratigraphic Column
Two Interpretations

Creation
Young Age View

Rocks and fossils
are snapshots of
living things deposited
at specific times
in Biblical history

Evolution
Geological Ages View

Rocks and fossils
represent evolution
throughout
geologic time

**Post Flood
Sediments**

Quaterary Rocks
Man
Tertiary Rocks
Mammals
Birds

2my

65my

**Cenozoic
"Recent Life"**

Secondary Rocks
Dinosaurs
Reptiles

**Flood
Sediments**

248my

**Mesozoic
"Middle Life"**

Primary Rocks
Trilobites
Marine Creatures
Amphibians

530my

**Paleozoic
"Early Life"**

Precambrian Rocks
Stromatolites

**Pre-flood
Sediments**

Protists Algae
Bacteria
Tiny Microorganisms

3800my

*The sedimentary rocks of the earth can be interpreted in at least two distinctly
different ways, outlined in the illustration above. Most people are only aware of
the evolutionary-geological ages model. Are both models reasonable? Which is
biblical?*   Erkel and Associates (Crozet, Va.)

God clearly shows Himself to be a *preserver of the righteous,* of those who believed His promises and walked with Him. Enoch (Genesis 5:21–24) was the first human being to be "taken up" to God without dying because he had persevered 365 years in close fellowship with God. Noah also was a righteous man who found favor with God (Genesis 6:8–10). Noah and his family were saved from the watery cataclysm to come.

Finally, the *Sovereign* God knew His ultimate plan for salvation of His people, and no evil acts of men could interfere. The line of Abel, carried on by righteous Seth, was to endure through the salvation of Noah and his son Shem, and on the appointed day the Savior of the world would come through that preserved bloodline.

What's Next?

God responded once more to man's sin, this time with a global cataclysm that is difficult for us to visualize. The following chapter will touch on what we think happened during this incredible divine judgment.

Consider the Concept

The first man, Adam, was possibly the most intelligent man to appear on the earth (until the time of Jesus Christ). Adam's descendants developed an advanced civilization. There is no place for the idea of a slowly evolving intelligence in the human race.

Questions to Ponder

- In your geology class, the rocks and fossils of the Primary sediments (also called "Paleozoic") would be linked to millions of years of evolution of early life forms. In the chapter you just read, a much different interpretation of those Primary sediments was given. Explain this interpretation to your geology professor.
- Adam lived 930 years. Is that a misprint? On the basis of the brief discussion in this chapter, how would you explain pre-Flood longevity to a scoffer?

- What do we learn about God from studying this epoch in earth history?
- Draw a picture (actually or mentally) of the pre-Flood world, with its floating forests, stromatolites, gymnospermous plants, and dinosaurs.
- Dinosaurs—always a popular subject. Explain something you learned about dinosaurs in this chapter that you didn't know previously.
- Is there anything in this chapter that surprised you? Got your attention? Made you want to learn more? What questions did this chapter provoke in your thinking?

A Verse to Remember

Therefore, just as sin entered the world through one man, and death through sin, in this way death spread to all men, because all sinned.

Romans 5:12

CHAPTER 11
THE FLOOD

THE apostle Peter wrote that a time would come when there would be people on earth who would "scoff" at the idea that Jesus Christ would come again. The passage further states that among their reasons for doubting a coming judgment is their denial of two facts from

---

2 PETER 3:3–7

First, be aware of this: scoffers will come in the last days to scoff, following their own lusts, saying, "Where is the promise of His coming? For ever since the fathers fell asleep, all things continue as they have been since the beginning of creation." They willfully ignore this: long ago the heavens and the earth existed out of water and through water by the word of God. Through these the world of that time perished when it was flooded by water. But by the same word the present heavens and earth are held in store for fire, being kept until the day of judgment and destruction of ungodly men.

---

earth history: Creation (because it would mean there was an authority over them with the right to judge) and the Flood (because it would mean that mankind had been judged at some point in the past).

That day has come, on campus and off. Most say there was no biblical flood at all. Others say that if there had been a biblical flood in Noah's day, it must have been merely a local flood.

News flash—Anyone who believes in the long age of the earth and cosmos, no matter how serious a Christian and biblical scholar, *must* deny a worldwide flood.

"How can that be," you ask? The academic discipline of geology, as taught in universities across the country and presented in museums, national parks, and popular literature, interprets the rock strata (layers) and fossils in such a way that, indeed, no evidence for a worldwide flood can be found. In the 1830s, Charles Lyell was instrumental in popularizing an interpretation of the rock strata known as *uniformitarianism* (or *anticatastrophism*). The principle of uniformity states that processes that occurred in past times produced the same results as similar processes do today (sedimentation, erosion, etc.). Therefore, Lyell concluded, the sediments that formed the rock layers were deposited slowly, as they are today. For example, if we look at the processes of sedimentation and erosion operating in our day-to-day world, one foot of sediment might take approximately five thousand to ten thousand years to be deposited. Since it is obvious that sedimentary rock layers are often found in thicknesses of thousands of feet, the conclusion would then be that the age of those rocks would number in millions of years. Furthermore, if the sediments are that old, the fossils found in them are remains of plants and animals that lived in the past, and the rock record gives us the history of life as it developed through many millions of years of earth history.

Even though many geologists today recognize the huge role catastrophic processes have played in earth history, the idea of long ages and the evolution of organisms has become firmly entrenched, and it prevails among the majority of geologists today. Our student, Scott, in a university geology class, would experience ridicule if he even suggested the concept of young age for the rock systems they study.

If one looks at the rock layers and fossils as representing billions of years of earth history, indeed a global flood must be denied because a flood of that magnitude would have to leave a record in the rocks, and if one (using the long-earth interpretation) looks to the part of the rock record estimated (by the conventional geologic time scale) at 4,500 years ago, he would see no evidence of a major flood.

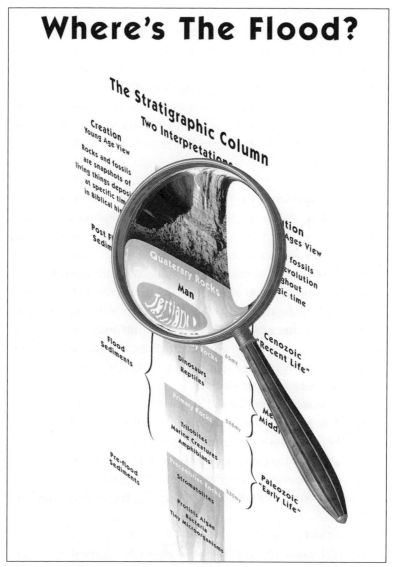

Where's The Flood?

The Stratigraphic Column
Two Interpretations

Creation
Young Age View

Rocks and fossils
are snapshots of
living things deposi...
at specific tim...
in Biblical his...

Post Fl...
Sedim...

Quaterary Rocks

Man

Tertiary

...ution
...ges View

...l fossils
...volution
...ghout
...ic time

Cenozoic
"Recent Life"

Flood
Sediments

Dinosaurs
Reptiles

...y Rocks 65my

Me...
Midd...

Primary Rocks 248my

Trilobites
Marine Creatures
Amphibians

Pre-flood
Sediments

Precambrian Rocks 530my

Stromatolites

Paleozoic
"Early Life"

Protists Algae
Bacteria
Tiny Microorganisms

Where's the Flood? In conventional geologic theory, evidence of a worldwide Flood occurring approximately 4,500 years ago would be obvious in "recent" layers of rock. According to their time scale, the evidence would be found in the Quaternary sediments. Since no such evidence is found in those strata, a global Flood is denied.

Erkel and Associates (Crozet, Va.)

Do you remember the principle of interpretation Scott learned early in this book? When an interpretation of scientific data contradicts the clear teaching of Scripture, it must be rejected, and another interpretation should be considered that is consistent with biblical truth. Since the conventional academic interpretation of the earth's rock layers denies a global flood, Scott needs to examine the evidence once more. Therefore, the first question we must consider in this chapter is "Does the Bible clearly teach a *global* flood in the days of Noah?"

Biblical Evidence for a Global Flood

Scripture makes it clear that the Flood in the days of Noah was global in extent; that is, it covered the whole face of the planet Earth.[1] Consider the following:

- God's stated purpose for the Flood was the destruction of all humans, land animals and birds, and even the earth itself (Genesis 6:5–7, 11–13, 17; 7:4). A global flood was the only way to fulfill this purpose, given the worldwide distribution of humans and animals. (When considering the longevity of humans, the population of the earth at the time of the Flood may have been close to the population of the world at the present time.)
- The ark would not have been necessary if the Flood had been local because man and animals simply could have moved to another region. Even with only hours of warning, for example, Lot was given a chance to escape from Sodom. In the case of the Flood, Noah may have been warned 120 years before the Flood (common understanding of Genesis 6:3).
- The description of the Flood utilizes inclusive terms. In the passage included in the box on the next page, note the key words *all, every, whole*. God seems to be telling us something here.
- The Hebrew word translated "flood" in the Genesis passages is *mabbul*. Other words are used to describe a variety

GENESIS 7:4, 11, 19–23

"Seven days from now I will make it rain on the earth 40 days and 40 nights, and I will wipe off the face of the earth every living thing I have made." . . . In the six hundredth year of Noah's life, in the second month, on the seventeenth day of the month, on that day all the sources of the watery depths burst open, the floodgates of the sky were opened, . . . Then the waters surged even higher on the earth, and all the high mountains under the whole sky were covered. The mountains were covered as the waters surged [above them] more than 20 feet. All flesh perished—creatures that crawl on the earth, birds, livestock, wildlife, and all creatures that swarm on the earth, as well as all mankind. Everything with the breath of the spirit of life in its nostrils—everything on dry land died. He wiped out every living thing that was on the surface of the ground, from mankind to livestock, to creatures that crawl, to the birds of the sky, and they were wiped off the earth. Only Noah was left, and those that were with him in the ark.

of floods elsewhere in Scripture, but this particular word is used only for the Flood in the days of Noah.

• God's promise—evidenced by the rainbow—declared that a flood would never again be sent to destroy the earth (Genesis 9:8–17). If the Flood of Noah's time had been local or even regional, each of the millions of local and regional floods that have occurred since the time of Noah would have broken that promise.

• The depth of the Flood waters require a global flood. "All the high mountains under the whole sky were covered" (Genesis 7:19). Long before the water was high enough to cover the mountains, the entire earth would have been covered.

• The length of the Flood (one year and ten days) was too long for a local or regional flood.

• The Bible refers to the Flood along with other global events. In 2 Peter 3:3–7, the apostle speaks of the coming judgment (certainly a global event) and Creation (another global event) before and after the Flood. Jesus Christ drew a similar comparison when He said that His return would be "As the days of Noah were" (Matthew 24:37).

Interpreting the Rocks in Light of Biblical Evidence

Because our student, Scott (and hopefully, our reader), understands that Scripture clearly teaches a global flood, he must now examine the evidence that has been interpreted conventionally to indicate billions of years of earth history with no record of a global flood. Could there be *another* viable interpretation of that data—one that is consistent with the biblical data?

Think for a moment about local flooding experienced in your area of the country or seen reported on TV: huge amounts of mud and other sediments deposited and piled up everywhere; things buried in the mud; whole hillsides washed away and deep gullies formed; the topography of the area completely rearranged. It is obvious that catastrophe—even a little "local flood"—changes the lay of the land.

Now let's expand our picture of a local flood to one that involves the entire world—not merely a rainstorm, but the presence of tectonic (relating to structural deformation of the earth's crust) events that go beyond anything we've ever seen. The evidence that should be found in the record of rocks and fossils should be enormous! In fact, this evidence might be expected to have a volume comparable to the volume of the earth's entire rock record. More and more of the earth's rock record is being reinterpreted, even by conventional geology, as having been formed catastrophically. Perhaps it is not unreasonable to claim that many of the earth's rocks were produced in *one* catastrophe—the Flood in the days of Noah. It would then follow that the rocks deposited during the year-long event would hold the remains of creatures who lived during that time and who were buried in the Flood.

Although some disagreement currently exists among young-age creationists about where in the rock record to put the Flood/post-Flood boundary, the authors of this book believe that the Primary (Paleozoic) and Secondary (Mesozoic) rocks were formed during the Flood.

From this viewpoint, instead of a record of evolution of one form of organism to another over billions of years, we see the record

The Stratigraphic Column
Two Interpretations

Creation
Young Age View

Rocks and fossils
are snapshots of
living things deposited
at specific times
in Biblical history

**Post Flood
Sediments**

**Flood
Sediments**

Evolution
Geological Ages View

Rocks and fossils
represent evolution
throughout
geologic time

**Cenozoic
"Recent Life"**

**Mesozoic
"Middle Life"**

**Paleozoic
"Early Life"**

Quaterary Rocks

2my

Birds

Secondary Rock

Dinosaurs
Reptiles

Primary Rocks

Trilobite

530my

Str...

Protists Algae
Bacteria
Tiny Microorganisms

3800my

Here's The Flood!

There's the Flood! The seekers for Flood evidence in the earlier illustration (p. 137) were looking in the wrong place in the column because their time scale prohibited them from seeing the massive evidence for the Flood in all the Primary and Secondary rocks. Erkel and Associates (Crozet, Va.)

of God's judgment and a portrait of the living things that were destroyed during that judgment.

It is an understatement to say that this reinterpretation of the rock record is not a popular idea in a world that has replaced the Creator's work with a godless theory of evolution and has denied that such a Creator would or could destroy the earth in judgment of sin. Yes, you will be ridiculed "out there" for even mentioning "Flood geology," even as the creationist interpretation gains more and more evidential support through continued research.

For the remainder of this chapter, we'll look at one of the major models proposed by creationist researchers to explain the data in a biblically affirming way. We'll also look at some of the evidence for the global Flood found in the rocks and fossils of the world.

How Did the Global Flood Come About? (or Where Did All That Water Come From?)

Those who would challenge the biblical record point out that if all the water were wrung out of all the clouds of the entire atmosphere, the sea level would be raised only about a half inch! Therefore, the critics argue, the Flood account must be wrong. There isn't enough water to do it, and even if there was, where did it all go?

Creationist geologists and physicists have been studying and proposing various models for how the Flood might have begun. (A model is a scientific framework of ideas used to help organize and understand facts in a meaningful way. A "scientific model" must be defended on the basis of evidence and experiments.) Some have suggested astronomical factors (a comet? a meteorite hitting the earth?), and others have proposed models that involve the collapse of a water vapor canopy. No consensus exists as yet.

In 1994, a group of three geologists (Steven Austin, Andrew Snelling, and Kurt Wise) and three geophysicists (John Baumgardner, D. Russell Humphreys, and Larry Vardiman) introduced a new model at the Third International Conference on Creationism. This model is based on current understanding of plate tectonics. The model is referred to as CPT (catastrophic plate tectonics). While it still remains a model, with much work still to be done, it does have great explanatory potential for establishing a biblical framework for understanding the Flood and much more. A simplified explanation of this model follows.

The Starting Point for the Model: Sea Floor Disturbance

Genesis 7:11 (see passage printed on the next page) refers to something called "all the sources of the watery depths" (also translated "fountains of the great deep" in KJV, NASB, RSV) existing on the pre-

Flood earth. They were possibly springs scattered across the earth's surface, both on continents and in the oceans. The Bible claims that all these fountains were broken up on a single day. Perhaps their breaking up resulted in the shattering of the earth's crust at numerous locations. We know that the current ocean crust is broken into a number of different pieces or plates. Perhaps it was early in the Flood that the earth's crust was broken into its present plates. The present and past motion of these plates is described in a theory called *plate tectonics*. The Flood model described in these pages is a modification of the conventional model of plate tectonics, called *catastrophic plate tectonics* (CPT).[2]

> ### GENESIS 7:11, 19
>
> *In the six hundredth year of Noah's life, in the second month, on the seventeenth day of the month, on that day all the sources of the watery depths burst open, the floodgates of the sky were opened, . . . Then the waters surged even higher on the earth, and all the high mountains under the whole sky were covered.*

What Is Plate Tectonics?

It would be impossible to understand CPT without knowing the basics of plate tectonics theory.

In 1859, a creationist named Antonio Snider proposed that all the continents were originally gathered together in one land mass and that crustal plates moved catastrophically during the Genesis Flood. However, his ideas were not considered or were readily dismissed. Darwin's *The Origin of Species* had been published the same year, and the idea of uniformitarian geology (slow processes over much time) as introduced by James Hutton and Charles Lyell had taken hold. For many years following, most geologists strongly held that the continents were stationary. However, beginning in the second decade of this century, a change in thought began. This change was accelerated in the 1960s as a result of scientific studies involving the mapping of the sea floors, the measuring of magnetic fields, and greater understanding of earthquakes through seismometers. Plate tectonics as a model of earth history was becoming accepted.

Basically, this is what plate tectonics theory claims:

- Most of the earth's crust can be classified into two types: basaltic and granitic. Since basaltic crust is denser (more compact), it sits lower in the earth's mantle, giving place for most of the world's water. Therefore it is called *oceanic crust*. Since granitic crust sits higher, it becomes the foundation for continents and is called *continental crust*.

The earth's crust consists of two different types: basaltic (ocean) and continental (granitic). Note above how the continental crust, being less dense, floats higher on the earth's mantle than does the denser ocean crust. This is why we have oceans.

Erkel and Associates (Crozet, Va.)

- The earth's surface is broken into a series of plates, focusing most geologic activity along plate boundaries. The plates in the world's oceans are spreading apart on some edges and sinking into the earth on others. The evidence that continents have moved in the past and that plate tectonics is responsible for most of that motion seems strongly evidenced in the geologic record.
- Since earthquakes result when rocks move against other rocks, earthquakes are found along all plate boundaries. Different plate boundaries do, however, have unique geo-

logical characteristics. Different plate motions produce unique landforms. There are basically three types of motion.

1. *When two plates move apart from each other.* As they move apart, molten rock from the mantle below rises and fills the space between the plates. As this molten rock cools, it hardens onto the edges of the separating plates as basalt, creating new oceanic crust. This happens, for example, at submerged mountain ranges, such as the Mid-Atlantic Ridge and East Pacific Rise.

2. *When two plates move toward each other.* If the colliding plates are both made of continental crust, the colliding edges are crumpled and uplifted, producing large curvilinear continental mountain ranges (e.g., the Himalayas and the Alps). If an oceanic plate is involved, an oceanic plate will sink under the other (called subduction). A deep trench forms where the plate subducts under the other, and molten rock from the sinking plate rises to the surface on the far side of the trench to form a chain of volcanoes (or volcanic islands if oceanic crust is there). The Aleutians, the Japanese, and the Indonesian Islands would be examples of volcanic islands formed in this way.

3. *When two plates are adjacent to and slip past each other.* Little more than earthquakes characterize this type of plate boundary; no mountains or trenches are formed. The San Andreas fault zone in California is an example of this kind of plate boundary.

It is generally accepted that a single supercontinent broke apart, with continental pieces moving apart to their current locations. This idea is based in part on the apparent fit of the eastern bulge of South America into the southwestern concavity of Africa, the corresponding correlation of the rock strata systems, and the crumple-type mountains found in North America and Western Europe.

Because uniformitarian evolutionary assumptions have been the basis for twentieth-century geology, plate tectonics theory suggests plates have always moved very slowly—about two to eighteen centimeters per year. At that rate, it would require approximately 100 million years to form an ocean basin or mountain range.

What Then Is Catastrophic Plate Tectonics?

Simply stated, in CPT we are talking not about "continental drift," but rather about "continental *sprint.*" Instead of referring to "inches per year," we're talking about "meters per *second.*" And we're also talking about something that created the global Flood.

Dr. John Baumgardner, working at the Los Alamos National Laboratory, has demonstrated from supercomputer modeling of processes in the earth's mantle that plate tectonics/continental drift can occur catastrophically.[3]

Before the Flood Began

We must begin with a basic understanding of the pre-Flood earth, which we think contained a core, mantle, and crust much as we have today. The core (the center of the earth) is very dense—probably from iron and nickel. It is the area from which we believe the magnetic field emanates. The core is divided into a solid inner core and a liquid outer core. The mantle, making up 70 percent of the volume of the earth, is made of solid silicate rocks, which amazingly have the property of behaving plastically under certain types of stress. The crust is a very thin outer shell, and it is the layer that is divided into plates of either oceanic or continental composition. Because there was both dry land and ocean from Day Three of Creation Week on, it is assumed continental and oceanic crust existed in the pre-Flood world very much as they do today.

Noah Is on the Ark: Flood, Day One—"Under the Surface"

It is not known what started the crustal plates in motion to begin the Flood. Many ideas have been suggested, including asteroid or comet hits such as we see in many popular "doomsday" movies today. God most likely had so prepared the earth for the

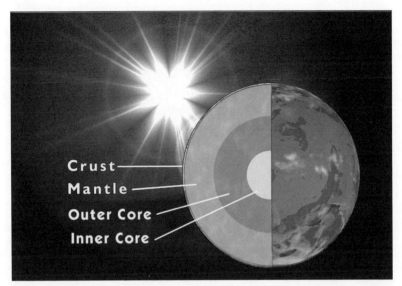

The earth's internal structure.   Erkel and Associates (Crozet, Va.)

Flood that it may not have taken much to set it in motion. Perhaps it is more than coincidence that when God slammed the door of the ark, the Flood began!

According to the CPT model, three events happened simultaneously and rapidly as the Flood began. Try to picture in your mind the three events happening at the same time.

1. *The ocean crust "takes a dive."* Visualize for a moment the area where the ocean crust and the continental crust come together. Remember, the crust of the continents is lighter and "floats" above the mantle, while the ocean crust is basaltic rock, which is more dense and sinks into the mantle. At the onset of the Flood, great lengths of ocean crust broke loose from the continental crust and began to dip into the mantle *(subduction)*. As oceanic crust broke loose, it dipped down along thousands of kilometers of pre-Flood continental margins. As it dove, it deformed the mantle material. The friction and deformation caused the temperature of the mantle material to increase, resulting

in the mantle material itself becoming thinner, speeding up the process. (Have you ever cooked with honey? When honey becomes warm, it becomes thinner and pours faster; but when it is cold, it is very thick. The crustal material dipping into the mantle experienced the same type of phenomenon.) In catastrophic plate tectonics theory it is believed that the sinking plates sped up until they were diving into the mantle at meters per second. This is called *runaway subduction.*

Now think about what was happening to the continents that were still attached to the other end of those runaway ocean plates. Those continents would have been pulled across the earth's surface toward the subduction zones at meters per second. Since the continental crust is lighter, once it got to the subduction zone it would not have been pulled all the way into the mantle, but the continent would have been taken on quite a ride nevertheless! As a result of this, continents would have broken up; continents would have collided; and enormous waves, earthquakes, and volcanoes would have resulted. It is believed, according to CPT theory, that essentially all the pre-Flood ocean floor was subducted into the mantle during the course of the Flood. (Evidence: present ocean crust and sediments seem to date from late-Flood or post-Flood times.)

2. *Circulation in both mantle and core.* Meanwhile, as the oceanic crust was swiftly dipping into the mantle, other processes were set in motion. Mantle material that was being pushed out of the way by the subducting crust had to go somewhere! Computer simulations suggest large-scale flow was induced throughout the entire mantle of the earth. (Evidence: seismic tomography studies seem to confirm that this has happened during the history of the earth.) Ultimately, the entire ocean floor was pulled down toward the core/mantle boundary. Even before the crust made it to the base of the mantle, cooler mantle material

Continental Crust

Oceanic Crust

Mantle

It has been observed on the present earth that when ocean crust comes together with continental crust, it slips below the crust and dips into the mantle (because it is denser than the continental crust). The Flood may have begun this way, with the subduction becoming a "runaway" process, pulling great lengths of ocean crust into the mantle. The ocean crust was then replaced by hot molten material from the mantle. Erkel and Associates (Crozet, Va.)

moved downward and cooled the outer core (which is a liquid) in an uneven way. This uneven cooling then initiated circulation patterns in the outer core.

It is known from studying magnetic fields that magnetic field lines are "tied" to the substance they are passing through. It is also known (for example, from generators) that moving magnetic field lines generate a changing electric current, and when one has a changing electric current, a weaker magnetic counterfield is created. According to the work of creationist physicist D. Russell Humphreys, circulation in the outer core created a weaker magnetic field oriented in the opposite direction from the earth's main field. This reversed field is transmitted to the outside

of the earth and is perceived on the surface as a drop in
magnetic field strength and a reversal of its direction.
Field reversals, and reversals of reversals, could happen
very quickly in this model. (Evidence: this model predicted that rapid magnetic field reversals might be found
in single layers of the "proper" thickness of cooling lava,
and this prediction has been confirmed.)[4]

Spreading, Subduction, and Mantle-Wide Flow

During the Flood, the sub-duction of the cooler ocean crust into the hot mantle would have caused circula-tion of the man-tle (gray arrows). The resulting tem-perature varia-tions at the base of the mantle would have stimulated circulation in the outer core (white arrows), resulting in rapid magnetic field reversals.

Erkel and Associates
(Crozet, Va.)

Crust

Mantle

Inner Core

Outer Core

3. *"Rains come down and waters come up."* While Noah was
    most likely unaware of diving ocean crust, circulating
    mantle and core, and even magnetic field reversals, he
    definitely was aware of this event. As the pre-Flood ocean
    floor dipped down into the mantle where plates came
    together, it was rapidly replaced by hot material from the
    mantle where the plates separated. The hot material com-

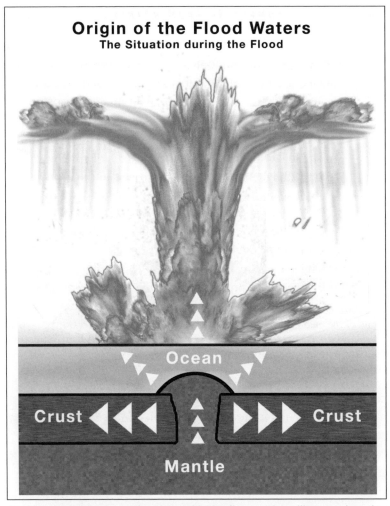

Origin of the Flood Waters
The Situation during the Flood

How did the Flood waters cover the earth? The diagram above illustrates how the molten material replacing the ocean floor would have served to raise sea level and displace water on the continents. Also, the hot molten material would have vaporized sea water and induced global rain. Erkel and Associates (Crozet, Va.)

ing from below, as it contacted ocean water, would have vaporized ocean water to produce a linear geyser of super-heated gases along the whole length of spreading bound-aries (a geyser effect—possibly the "fountains of the great deep"?). As it cooled, the water—both that vaporized from ocean water and that released from magma—would have fallen as an intense global rain. It is this geyser-produced rain that is believed primarily responsible for the rain from the "windows of heaven" that remained a source of water for up to 150 days of the Flood (Genesis 7:24; 8:2).

But how then was the water able to cover the continents, including the high mountains, all over the world? If water simply evaporated from the ocean and fell back in again, sea level would have remained unchanged. In the CPT model, the replacement of cold ocean crust with more expanded hot ocean crust raised the ocean bottom. The rising ocean bottom displaced water onto the continents, raising sea level perhaps more than a mile over antediluvian levels. This produced the Flood itself. These waters raised the ark upon their surface and ultimately passed it over the tops of the highest antediluvian mountains.

The End of the Flood

While Noah and his family were floating on the water, caring for animals and waiting on the Lord, significant geological events were occurring "under the surface." The Flood survivors would soon face a world much altered in every way.

When all the antediluvian ocean crust had disappeared into the mantle, the ocean crust that replaced it was still warm. Being warm, it was less dense than the mantle, so gravity did not pull it into the mantle below, and horizontal plate motions on the surface ground to a halt. Without the plates separating quickly at the spreading lines, molten mantle material was no longer contacting sea water, and the earth-ringing "fountains of the great deep" ceased to spout. They were "stopped" (Genesis 8:2). Without the mid-ocean fountains supplying water, the "windows of Heaven" also ceased (Genesis 8:2), making it possible for the earth to return to a normal water cycle of evaporating water and condensing water vapor from clouds.

It took a few weeks for the last of the pre-Flood crust to drop to the bottom of the mantle. Once this happened, the mantle motions slowed and ceased. (Since it has now been only 4,500 years or so since the Flood, temperature differences in the mantle still show up with seismic tomography.) The ocean crust cooled and shrank as it did so. The Flood waters were able to return gradually to the ocean basins. As the water subsided, the ark was set upon the "mountains of Ararat" (Genesis 8:4).

Once the rapid horizontal motion stopped, cooling increased the density of the new ocean floor, producing gradually deepening oceans. This and other geological adjustments took the Flood waters back into the ocean basins and eventually produced our current sea level and ocean configurations.

Is This the Final Word?

Do we know that catastrophic plate tectonics is the final word on what happened in the Flood? No. This model represents new thinking about those events, and it may be modified greatly or even discarded for another model in the future.

So then, why bother? Does it really matter whether or not we know how it all happened?

On one hand, it doesn't matter. We have absolute truth that God brought a watery judgment upon the whole earth; how He did it we may not know this side of heaven. But on the other hand, He has given us minds and has encouraged us to search out truth in order to come to know Him better. Psalm 111:2 tells us: "The LORD's works are great, studied by all who delight in them." As we study His works, we see His power, His holiness, His mercy, His provision, His sovereignty. He indeed was King at the Flood, and this event gives us an important framework for understanding our world and our lives today.

Can We See Flood Evidence in the Rocks and Fossils Today?

Once the naturalistic scales that cover our eyes drop off and we look through biblical eyeglasses, tantalizing observations of this event 4,500 years ago appear before our eyes. The Flood was a geological catastrophe, and it left its evidence everywhere.

Following are just a few evidences that can be observed from the
rocks and fossils of our world:

- *In the Rock Layers.* Primary and Secondary (Paleozoic and
  Mesozoic) sediments are often deposited in great thicknesses, with remarkable uniform compositions, spread
  over very large areas, and frequently displaced hundreds
  of miles from their source area. For example, the Chinle
  Formation covers 175,000 square miles in Utah, Northern
  Colorado, Northern Arizona, and New Mexico. The
  Morrison Formation (with lots of dinosaurs) covers
  400,000 square miles from Texas to Canada.

- *In the Currents.* On the present earth, sediments are being
  carried toward and within the ocean in all directions.
  Anything that indicates the direction of currents (such as
  ripple marks) should show a random pattern on every
  continent. But evidence suggests otherwise.[5] It is as if during the deposition of Primary and Secondary rocks, the
  currents on the earth were consistently in one direction—
  more or less east to west.

- *In the Fossils.* If the fossils were deposited rapidly in a
  global flood, they should produce a very different record
  than that predicted by other models of earth history. If
  the earth's sediments were deposited while organisms
  were evolving (as many alternate theories suggest), then a
  vertical sequence of fossils should document that transition. Organisms should be found in the order they
  evolved. Intermediates should be found in layers between
  their ancestors and descendants. And species should be
  seen changing up through the record. Just as a branching
  tree can become broad only after it has produced many
  branches, so also evolving life can only generate markedly
  different biological forms after it has produced many
  species.[6] In Flood theory, however, the organisms that
  lived on the earth at a particular point in time were rapidly buried, community by community. Therefore, organ-

isms should not be found in the order evolution predicts. Intermediates should not be found in layers between proposed ancestors and descendants. Organisms should not change up through the fossil column, and markedly different organisms should be evidenced from the very beginning of the record.

In fact, it is rare that organisms are found in the order predicted by evolutionary theory. Intermediates are only very rarely found between proposed ancestors and descendants. Organisms usually show no change up through the fossil record. And wide amount of variation (disparity) in the form of organisms appears at the very *beginning* of the fossil record, usually before the number of species rises. This observation challenges the idea of a tree branching out; it actually seems to turn the tree upside down!

Another observation about the fossil record: All other things being equal, a lower rate of the deposition of sediments, as assumed in evolutionary theory, should preserve fewer fossils. Under these conditions, much more time is available for organisms to destroy the layers of sediment; therefore, fine sedimentary layering should be rarer. Yet the fossil record has an abundance of both well-preserved fossils and finely layered sediments over the whole earth.

Also, if the fossil record is a documentation of hundreds of millions of years of time, then the approximately 250,000 fossil species documented to date would have to be an extremely low percentage of all the species that have ever lived. In contrast, the rapid deposition rate of the Flood would probably have resulted in a very large percentage of fossil species being preserved. Our observation is that a very large percentage of modern species have a fossil record. This suggests that the fossil record is as good as young-age creationism suggests and not as poor as alternate theories might suggest.

- *Folded, Twisted Rocks.* Once a rock has hardened, it is very difficult to bend and twist it without breaking it. Yet throughout the rock record we find countless examples of rock that has been bent and twisted as if it were soft spaghetti. According to conventional radiometric dating, these rock layers are often separated by many millions of years. It is much more plausible to understand the twisting and bending in light of a year-long catastrophic event involving rocks not yet fully hardened.[7]

How could this rock bend without breaking? In this photo taken in the extreme eastern Grand Canyon, we observe strata of the Tapeats Sandstone Formation. Intense forces caused once-horizontal sandstone to be turned tightly into vertical orientation. Note the upwarp on the right side of the picture. People provide scale.
Photo by Steve Austin, courtesy of Institute for Creation Research

- *Lack of Erosion between Sedimentary Layers.* Between layers of rock everywhere we see flat contact lines, as if one layer had been deposited rather quickly upon the layer that preceded it. Yet the conventional interpretation often places "time gaps" of millions of years between each layer. Millions of years of erosion should be visible between these deposits if indeed these were actual time gaps. It seems much more plausible to view these sedimentary deposits as occurring within the time framework of a biblical flood.[8]

This photo was taken along the Bright Angel Trail in the Grand Canyon. In it we see the contact between the cream-colored Coconino Sandstone above and the red siltstone of the Hermit Formation beneath. No evidence of prolonged weathering or erosion can be noted between the two layers.

Photo by Steve Austin, courtesy of Institute for Creation Research

- *Mountains.* If the earth is very old, than the earth's eroded fold—belt mountains—is very old. We are taught from many sources that the Appalachian Mountains, for example, are hundreds of millions of years old. If that were the case, then the only geologic changes that should be occurring would be erosion slowly taking off the top of the mountains and the minor rebounding of the mountains because of this loss of mass. But if the Appalachians were formed by continental collision early in the Flood, they were formed only thousands of years ago, and the top of the mountains was eroded off soon thereafter. Since it should take the earth's surface some twenty-five thousand years to respond fully to quick vertical changes, the mountains that were formed and shaved off during the Flood should still be recovering. This would explain the large number of earthquakes associated with the Appalachians. Young-age creation theory leaves more room for this than alternative models.

There are still questions and challenges to the understanding of earth history in relation to the Flood of Noah. Much research is being done currently, with more needed. Great opportunities are available for Christian students in geology and other sciences to participate in origins research in areas that could honor the Creator.

Summary: What We Learn about the Artist from What He Has *Done*

Obviously, we see incredible power in forces that affected the entire earth and cosmos. God touched the mountains, and they trembled. *God's power* goes beyond anything we can even imagine.

We also see Him as *Judge*. He is a *Holy God* and must judge sin.

He is a God who *keeps His promises*. He warns, patiently waits, and then is faithful to do what He says He will do.

He is a God who *takes care of His own*. Noah and his family "rode out the storm" while incredible catastrophe was all around them.

What's Next?

As Noah and his family stepped off the ark, they entered a completely new world—the third radically new world in Creation history. Imagine it! No plant, animal, mineral, spring, river, mountain, or even continent was where it had been before. Even the moon looked different.[9] In the years to follow, more changes would occur as organisms repopulated the earth, the seas gradually returned to their basins, the earth sank convulsively or rose to proper levels, and the climate tried to even out earth temperatures.

This altered world is the one of *our* age. In the next two chapters we will survey a few characteristics of the first centuries of our present world: first, the early post-Flood history of the earth and its organisms, then the early post-Flood history of man.

Consider the Concept

A person who is thinking clearly cannot accept both the concept of billions of years of earth history revealed in the rock record *and* the biblical teaching of a worldwide flood in the days of Noah. The two are contradictory thoughts.

Questions to Ponder

- Catastrophic plate tectonics . . . whew! Reread the chapter's discussion of plate tectonics theory and CPT. Now try to explain in simple terms how the rapid movement of plates could have caused the Flood.
- What evidences can we observe today that point to a worldwide flood? Many were given in this chapter. Choose the ones you found most compelling, and be ready to explain them to your geology teacher.
- Is there anything in this chapter that surprised you? Got your attention? Made you want to learn more? What questions did this chapter provoke in your thinking?
- What do we learn about God from what He has done in the Flood?

A Verse to Remember

You covered it with the deep
as if it were a garment;
the waters stood above the mountains.
At Your rebuke the waters fled;
at the sound of Your thunder they hurried away—
mountains rose and valleys sank—
to the place You established for them.
You set a boundary they cannot cross;
they will never cover the earth again.

Psalm 104:6–9

CHAPTER 12
THE POST-FLOOD WORLD

IT must be noted for the sake of our college student, Scott (and for all who read this book), that the subject of this chapter would not be a part of his formal education. His textbooks would be silent regarding the effects of a universal flood because such a flood is denied. While modern geology observes the same data—rocks and fossils—it interprets this data from an entirely different framework. However, when a biblical framework is considered, the period following the Flood is a fascinating one. It has important implications for the sciences of geology, paleontology, biology, and geography.

What would it have been like to leave the ark and begin life in a world that had been totally changed by the Flood? Our informed imaginations have to fill in where the Bible is silent as we think about how *we* would have reacted to the destruction and desolation that must have been evident. Children's picture books of the ark's survivors coming aground to a beautiful world with flowers growing, sun shining, and birds singing is undoubtedly *not* the world they encountered. Many questions would have been on their minds as they disembarked: *What direction should we go from this mountainous area? Where will we sleep? What will we eat in the months to come? How do we make a beginning in this strange place?*

In the Book of Genesis, the period from Noah until God's call of Abram covers approximately three hundred to five hundred years. In chapter 13, we will focus on Noah and his descendants and their response to God during this period. But first we will consider this new world they encountered and some of the challenges they must have faced.

Still Feeling the Effects

Consider once more what was happening while Noah and his family were protected in the ark. Colliding plates produced new mountains in a time period of days, and rapidly moving Flood waters then eroded them in weeks. Continents were pressed down by thousands of feet of water and then uncovered only months later. Earthquakes moved rocks up and down by thousands of feet in seconds, minutes, and hours. Mid-ocean ridges rose and sank, while trenches sank and rose in weeks and months. By the end of the Flood, rocks and plates everywhere across the planet were sitting either too high or too low. Just as ice cubes pushed beneath the water or pulled above its surface return to their proper position, so also the earth's rocks following the Flood began rebounding to their appropriate locations.

Rebounding Phenonmenon

But the earth's mantle does not allow this to happen in seconds, as is the case with ice cubes in water. It is estimated that rocks require about twenty-five thousand years in order to return to their proper position. Although most of this motion would probably have occurred in the first one thousand years or so after the Flood, some of this vertical motion would be occurring even today.

Earthquakes

Observation: Today there are many active earthquakes in mountain chains—both in mountains such as the Appalachians, which are considered very "old," and in rising mountains, such as the Tetons.

An earthquake is the vibration of the earth's surface that follows a release of energy in the earth's crust. Most earthquakes are caused by dislocations in the crust, which are usually found where plates meet. After the Flood, conditions for earthquake activity were optimal.

During the Flood, when all the cold ocean crust had sunk beneath the earth's surface, horizontal movement of plates ceased for a time. In the months, years, and centuries that followed, the new ocean crust cooled. In areas farthest from the mid-ocean ridge, the crust had cooled for the longest time, leaving it denser (more compact) in those locations. In areas closer to the mid-ocean ridge, the crust was warmer, buoying the crust upward, preventing the rapid sinking that occurred during the Flood. The process continues even today. Cooling of the crust continues. Gravity is pulling colder crust slabs downward, explaining the extensional earthquakes found in the center of the short subducted portions of large ocean plates. The

• •

The ice cubes are being forcefully held down in the left photo. Once released, they rebound to their proper position. If pulled up to a higher position, the ice cubes would similarly rebound (downward) to their proper position. This same principle applies to earth rocks "floating" on the earth's mantle. Chunks of earth crust that were pushed too high or too low during the Flood will rebound to their proper positions in the years following the Flood. Because of how viscous (thick) the earth's mantle is, many crustal pieces are even at this time still rebounding from the event 4,500 years ago.   Erkel and Associates (Crozet, Va.)

small plate motions that occur as a result of this sinking of colder crust explain the position, depth, and direction of motion of most of the world's earthquakes.

It may be that the restarting of limited plate motion began even before the Flood was over. At first this motion—combined with the vertical motion of rocks and slabs that were out of position—may have been rather dramatic. Many mountains were actually broken off their foundations and bounced across the earth's surface for dozens of miles and more. As time went on, this energy would have lessened.

Observation: Mountains have been found that are "root-less," indicating they had been severed off and moved across large distances from their original location (where their "roots" have been discovered). This phenomena has not been explained in alternative models of earth history. Incredible amounts of energy appear to have been unleashed, for example, around the San Andreas Fault in the past. This model would also explain why the frequency and size of earthquakes has been decreasing since it has become possible to measure them.

Volcanoes

In addition to plate movement, rocks that had been quickly buried in the earth's interior during the Flood began to melt, causing rising magma (melted rock) to punch its way to the surface and generate volcanoes. Large numbers of extremely explosive volcanoes would be expected during the last part of the Flood and the period immediately following. In the years following the Flood, less and less magma would have been generated because the Flood-buried rocks would have been cooling. Volcanoes would therefore have decreased in size and frequency.

Observations: Huge volumes of volcanic ash are found in Secondary and Tertiary sediments. This ash created ideal conditions for fossil burial and preservation, such as for Arizona's Petrified Forest and many of the vertebrate bone beds.

The most explosive type of volcanoes (called rhyolytic
volcanoes) disappeared in the Tertiary sediments (believed
to be post-Flood). Volcanoes have decreased in size and fre-
quency up to the present.

In young-age creation geology, the earthquakes and volcanoes
of the present are largely residual effects of the Flood, meaning that
the earth is still recovering from the effects of the Flood.

Today, we still experience many natural disasters, with the
resulting death and suffering. Have you ever stopped to consider
these to be a consequence of the Flood—divine judgment on man's
sin? Man, then, is responsible not only for the moral evil and natural biological evil of disease and death, but for natural geological
evil as well.

After the Flood: Climate

It's Wet Out Here!

Obviously, the hot ocean crust produced during the Flood
released a huge amount of heat. Although much of the heat was
probably jettisoned into space, some of the heat was directly
absorbed by the ocean water. Therefore, it is probable that the ocean
water was very warm by the end of the Flood.

What would be the effect of warm oceans? First, a lot of water
would evaporate into the atmosphere. Since continents cool more
quickly at night than oceans do, cool air from the continents would
tend to move over the oceans to take the place of the warm air rising from their surface. The warm, moisture-laden air would then
move over the continents to replace the air moving off to sea. This
moist air over the continents would be cooled, causing condensa-
tion and precipitation—*lots* of precipitation. Evaporation off a surface cools that surface (as evaporation of sweat cools our skin).
Evaporation of water from the ocean after the Flood gradually
cooled the oceans. As they cooled, less precipitation was generated,
and the entire earth gradually dried.[1]

This photo from space reveals a large hurricane seen over North America. Following the Flood, the effects of warm moisture-laden air from the ocean moving over the cool continents would have caused much precipitation and possibly hurricanes many times larger than this. Courtesy of NOAA

The young-age creationist Flood model suggests that the oceans heated up during the Flood and cooled down in the centuries following.

> *Observation: Study of the shells of single-celled marine organisms seem to indicate an increase in ocean temperatures through the Primary and Secondary (Flood sediments) and a decrease during the Tertiary (post-Flood).*

What would be the result of high precipitation? Following are some expectations:

- *Sheet Erosion over the Earth's Surface.* If the water came down fast enough, it would not channel itself into streams but rather flow in sheets over the earth's surface.

In some areas this would erode sediments and rocks in a planar (flat, level) fashion.

Observation: Widespread leveling off of rocks is found in Tertiary (post-Flood) sediments.

- *Sheet Deposition of Sediments.* As water slows down, it begins to drop out the sediments it carries. The water that eroded in sheets on steep slopes deposits sediment in sheets on more horizontal slopes. Sediments would be carried further with higher rainfall rates. As precipitation lessened, deposits would occur over progressively smaller areas.

Observation: Nearly flat wedges of sediment are found in Tertiary sediments, becoming less extensive up through the Tertiary and into the Quaternary. Large fans of river material, such as the famous sediment fans of Death Valley and the great deltas of the world, were probably mostly formed in this way.

- *Lakes.* Many lakes would form as a result of the high precipitation.

Observation: Many lakes are found in post-Flood sediments. Examples include Fossil Lake, which preserved the famous fossil fish of Fossil Butte National Monument; Lake Manly, which used to be found in Death Valley; and Lake Bonneville, of which the Great Salt Lake is a small, evaporated remnant.

- *Canyons.* When lakes fill up and overflow, they tend to cut quickly (in hours) through whatever dam holds them in place, whether natural or man-made. The same precipitation that generated the post-Flood lakes may have overflowed many of them. This water would have quickly cut through the dams, rapidly drained the lakes, and left behind spectacular canyons.

Observation: Evidence has been found upstream of the Grand Canyon for the existence of a large lake that breached its dam and cut the canyon in the process.[2]

Breached Dam and Canyon Formation

How was the Grand Canyon formed? A series of large lakes are believed to have existed east and north of the Kaibab Upwarp (diagram A). The catastrophic drainage of a lake in eastern Arizona (diagram B) first created a notch and channel through the Kaibab Upwarp. Then catastrophic drainage of each of the upstream lakes in sequence (diagram C) further eroded the Grand Canyon to its current shape and established what is now the upper Colorado River basin.

Courtesy of ICR and Erkel and Associates (Crozet, Va.)

It may turn out that all the world's canyons were cut during catastrophic floods that occurred within the first one thousand years following the great Flood. Most of the rivers of the present earth may actually be flowing through remnant canyons cut during the post-Flood period of earth history.

- *Caves.* It may also turn out that most of the world's caves were carved out during this dynamic period of earth history.

The Drying Out Process Begins

As rainfall decreased, the earth dried. And with drying came a change in vegetation.

Observation: Genesis 13:10–11 informs us that in Abraham and Lot's day, only a few centuries after the Flood, the Dead Sea region was "well-watered everywhere like the LORD's garden" and thus attractive to Lot. Today that same area is a desert. Another example is provided in Numbers 13:23–27, when the now-desert land of Canaan was reported to be an incredibly fertile land that was "flowing with milk and honey."

The drying of the earth caused water-loving woodlands to dwindle worldwide, gradually replacing them with extensive grasslands. Eventually, further drying generated the world's deserts that we see today.[3]

Observation: The Sahara Desert has evidence of rivers and forests beneath its wind-blown sands.[4] The Sphinx of Egypt shows signs of being eroded by rainfall, while younger Egyptian edifices, like the pyramids, only have evidence of wind erosion.[5]

A Variety of Climate Zones

The evaporation of water from the oceans finally cooled the oceans after the Flood. For most of this period, though, the continents would have been substantially cooler than the oceans. Traveling from the ocean inland, the temperature would have dropped rapidly. As a result of this temperature structure, different plants and animals probably thrived closer to the ocean than inland. And since the temperature changed quickly as one went inland, the communities were probably geographically narrow and overlapped with adjacent communities.

Observation: Fossils of Tertiary plant communities found near the continental margins tend to have a mixture of plants with different climatic tolerances.

After the Flood: An Ice Advance

Eventually, the world's oceans cooled sufficiently for precipitation to come down at high altitudes and latitudes as snow. Since it came down so quickly, summer warmth in many places was not able to melt all the snow that had fallen the previous winter. As a result, snow built up and was compacted in some places into ice, which in turn accumulated into huge ice sheets. Eventually, the ice became so thick that it flowed under its own weight, surging over areas where there was no ice.

Evidence: Computer modeling studies that begin with a warm ocean suggest that the ice accumulated in the places we know it actually did accumulate and that this happened in the matter of a few centuries. This modeling seems to be the only modeling that successfully produces ice sheets where we know they were. The ice accumulation and melting of these models is of course too rapid for alternate theories—theories that also cannot explain how the ocean became warm in the first place.

Because the ice probably surged out in a couple of decades and then melted in another couple of decades, this rapid buildup and surging of ice is more appropriately called an *Ice Advance* rather than an *Ice Age.*

The Ice Advance model has a lot of advantages because it explains most of the same evidence given by conventional Ice Age theory but goes beyond that. For example, Ice Advance theory suggests that there was only one ice advance, with multiple surges. It also claims that the ice was much thinner and did not remain as long as conventional theory believes. Therefore, it more easily explains how there could be ice-free regions, such as around Appleton, Wisconsin—places that glaciers completely surrounded but never covered with ice.

Also, if thick ice had remained on the continent for a long time, it would have bowed the continent down under the weight. Since it may take the earth some twenty-five thousand years to recover completely from being depressed in this fashion, it should still be rebounding. However, most of Ohio, Indiana, and Illinois show little to no rebound—as if the ice was either very thin or it was not there very long.

After the Flood: A "Wild and Changing World" of Living Things

When we visualize the animals disembarking the ark after the Flood, we are influenced by the pictures in children's books of happy giraffes frolicking with poodles, leopards, and lions. Actually, we would probably be surprised at the animals we would find beginning life after the deluge. We need to remember that the organisms represented on the ark were "kinds," a more restricted term than the multitudes of species that have developed over the centuries. Although every modern and descendant animal had a representative on the ark, he probably didn't look a lot like his present-day relative.

Animals and plants experienced an explosion of change in the centuries following the Flood. The Bible describes some modern species existing within one thousand years of the Flood (donkeys and camels in Genesis 12:16; lions in Job 4:10–11). The fossil record suggests that almost all modern species were in place soon after the Ice Advance, which likely occurred within a thousand years after the Flood. The archaeological record has modern species of plants and animals represented in human art and preserved in archaeological sites early in the development of post-Babel cultures. All this would suggest that new species must have arisen at a stunningly high rate in the centuries following the Flood.

"Isn't this evolution you're describing?" you might ask. No. Evolutionary theory as taught today could not possibly accomplish this feat in the short amount of time we're talking about, nor could the change have occurred through common evolutionary mechanisms. We are speaking here of yet undiscovered built-in mechanisms of change that allowed these organisms to change quickly and dramatically following the Flood.

Let's go back to the beginning again and ponder the character of the God Who created life in this world. He created organisms knowing they would be facing incredible challenges following the Fall and the Flood. He designed them in such a way that they could adapt to changing world conditions.

AGEs

Creation biologists are only beginning to investigate these change mechanisms, so by the time this book is in print there will be more developments, and what is said here will probably be obsolete (as is true with most books on science). There has been proposed an interesting theory called *altruistic genetic elements (or AGEs)*. "Altruistic" refers to the principle of sacrifice of self in the interest of others, and this name gives a hint of the action of these elements.[6]

Altruistic genetic elements are pieces of DNA (genetic elements) that are designed to multiply and move around, both within and between organisms. Many of these genetic elements function something like switches for genes that are already there. A given genetic element might affect one or more genes. It might act on genes that are already in use—speeding them up, slowing them down, or turning them off. It might act on genes that have not yet been active, turning them on.

Switching on genes—especially genes that affect a cascade of other genes—can change organisms a lot—and quickly! Since these genetic elements were created by God to benefit the organisms, they reproduce themselves and are spread around for the benefit of the earth's organisms. Thus explains the reason for the name "altruistic."

AGEs may provide an explanation for several interesting features in the DNA of organisms not explained well by other theories. Since we can now examine DNA in minute detail, we may soon be able to recognize genes that either no longer function because they have been turned off by AGEs or have never (yet) been turned on by AGEs. Many exciting opportunities for research await those students who are interested in biology and desire to know more about the Master Designer through what He has made.

What Post-Flood Fossils Teach Us

As we examine the fossil record, we see that in perhaps as few as three centuries, scores of new species arose within most mammal baramins, and thousands of species arose within many of the insect and plant baramins. (Remember, the word "baramin" from chapter 6? It refers to the original "created kinds.") Many of these animals would become extinct by the catastrophic and changing environments after the Flood, but many others would survive for a time—long enough to produce new generations of different organisms.

No, this isn't "evolution"; it is change totally within a created kind, and it is consistent with the record of Scripture. If you want a fancy name, it is called *intrabaraminic diversification.* It illustrates in a grand way how the Creator God enabled his creatures to adapt and spread out and fill the earth as He commanded them to do.

Observations from the fossil record found in the sediments of the Tertiary and Quaternary (all considered post-Flood sediments) give us some interesting documentation of this wild and changing world.

Observation: Mammal species seem to increase in size through the Tertiary and into Quaternary sediments.

During this period the world was cooling. Bulkier animals are better able to survive in cooler environments.

Observation: Changes in teeth of some mammals (horses, camels, rabbits, and elephants, to name a few) are found in the Tertiary and Quaternary sediments.

The drying of the earth had its effects. Grasslands spread at the expense of woodlands. Baramins that seem to exclusively browse on trees and shrubs low in the Tertiary come to be represented in the higher Tertiary by organisms that prefer grass (grazers). Their teeth stood higher above the gumline and were flatter and larger—all useful in chewing grass.

Observation: Vestigial structures and genetic throwbacks.

Vestigial structures are structures in organisms that had a strong function in the past but now seem to have reduced function or no function at all. (Hip and leg bones that appear in some fetal sperm whales are vestigial structures, which suggest that whales in the past had hind limbs.) Genetic throwbacks are past structures that appear spontaneously in a small percentage of offspring in the present. (Horses born with multiple toes suggest they might have descended from horses in the past that had more than the single toe of modern horses.) Evolutionary theory promotes the finding of these structures as evidence of evolution because it sees organisms as constantly evolving new structures and phasing out old structures. Young-age creation theory recognizes that intrabaraminic changes (changes within the created kind) would have occurred, including the loss or partial loss of structures. It would suggest, however, that these changes occurred within the last few thousand years.

Rather than evidence for evolution over long ages, the presence of vestigial structures and genetic throwbacks suggests that the transformations were not made long ago. Complex structures that provide no advantage to the organisms tend to get eliminated by natural selection, and the genetic information needed to build them tends to get destroyed rapidly by mutation. The existence of vestigial structures and genetic throwbacks is more easily explained by young-age creation claims that it occurred only thousands of years ago, rather than conventional claims that it occurred tens of millions of years ago.

• •

The sediments of the Tertiary and Quaternary rocks are believed by many young-age creationists to be post-Flood sediments.

Erkel and Associates (Crozet, Va.)

Post-Flood
Sedimentary Rocks

The Stratigraphic Column
Two Interpretations

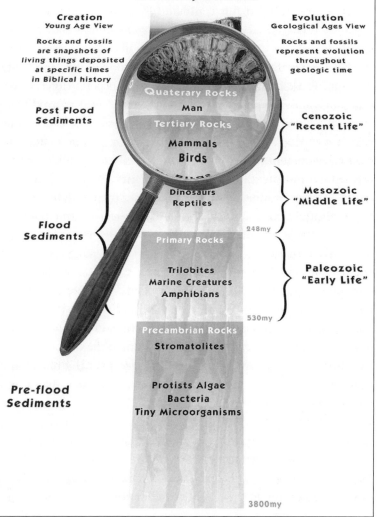

Creation
Young Age View

Rocks and fossils
are snapshots of
living things deposited
at specific times
in Biblical history

**Post Flood
Sediments**

**Flood
Sediments**

**Pre-flood
Sediments**

Evolution
Geological Ages View

Rocks and fossils
represent evolution
throughout
geologic time

Quaterary Rocks
Man
Tertiary Rocks
Mammals
Birds

**Cenozoic
"Recent Life"**

Dinosaurs
Reptiles

**Mesozoic
"Middle Life"**

248my

Primary Rocks

Trilobites
Marine Creatures
Amphibians

**Paleozoic
"Early Life"**

530my

Precambrian Rocks
Stromatolites

Protists Algae
Bacteria
Tiny Microorganisms

3800my

Multiplying and Filling the Earth

After the Flood, God's command to once again be fruitful, multiply, and fill the earth extended to all the survivors of the Flood (the water-loving organisms outside the ark as well as land-dwelling organisms inside the ark). As we'll see in the next chapter, the animals did a far better job of obeying this command than did the humans.

How they fulfilled this command involves the science of *biogeography,* a science of where organisms live and how they come to live there.

Remember the description of the pre-Flood world? In chapter 10 you read about floating forests, gymnosperm forests with dinosaurs, and stromatolite reefs. Since the Flood destroyed many of the pre-Flood communities, and the oceans of the catastrophe-ridden post-Flood world were probably far too choppy to allow for the redevelopment of the floating forest, it is easy to understand the extinction or near-extinction of all the plants and animals of those environments. In addition, the new continents seem to have lacked the hydrothermal margins (stromatolite reefs) of the pre-Flood world, and that would force hydrothermal organisms (those that flourish in hot water) to survive in small, isolated places in the post-Flood world (such as mid-ocean ridges and geysers). The slower reproductive rate of gymnospermous plants probably led to their being crowded out by competition, and the lack of this favorite food of dinosaurs probably contributed to their extinction (perhaps ultimately at the hand of humans who hunted them).

How did the surviving organisms spread over the planet after the Flood? There was likely an enormous migration. The warm, post-Flood oceans created a wet tropical climate along the shorelines of the world for those organisms that loved tropical temperatures to follow. The cool, dry continents generated parallel zones of subtropical, warm-temperate, and cool-temperate climate bands inside the coastal tropical bands. Thus, the animals had their choice of routes according to their preferred climate.

As the earth cooled and precipitation began accumulating in continental glaciers, the sea level dropped, opening up land bridges across shallow seas, such as the Bering Strait between Asia and North America, the English Channel between England and France, and much of the ocean among the Indonesian islands. These land bridges enabled routes for migration of the animals.

Since some of the plants of the present world can float for decades (like the Douglas fir on Spirit Lake near Mount Saint Helens), plant rafts may have floated about on the world's oceans for many years following the Flood. These rafts may have provided transport for many organisms across the oceans in the post-Flood world.[7] Faster-moving organisms (such as marsupials, which don't have to stop as long to care for young) may have been the first to ride these rafts over and colonize island continents (like Australia and Antarctica—even South America, which has only recently joined North America). By the time slower organisms made it to key locations, the plant rafts may have been destroyed.

Summary: What We Learn about the Creator/Artist from What He Has Done

To name just a few:

- Every time the people of the earth experience an earthquake, a volcano, or a hurricane, they are reminded that God judges sin. They remember His awesome power.
- The One Who brought judgment also protected His people through the judgment, allowing the earth to be renewed and diverse life to continue. He protected Noah and his descendants through fire and earthquake, leading them to places of safety.
- The triune God of diversity provided a variety of climates and conditions to support a variety of organisms.
- Our altruistic God, Who sacrificed Himself in the interest of others, provided altruistic genetic elements designed to benefit the organisms He created.

- Our God of abundance and beauty abundantly refilled the earth with beauty and variety.

What's Next?

While the earth was recovering from the Flood and organisms were repopulating the earth, man was not recovering quite so well—or obeying quite so completely. Perhaps man didn't believe God's promise that He would not destroy the earth by water again. Perhaps man was afraid to move out into an unknown new world in catastrophic mode. Whatever the reasons, man's disobedience led to another catastrophe—one that people don't often consider—another judgment that had widespread effects and forced mankind to fulfill the mandate given them.

Consider the Concept

Natural disasters (earthquakes, volcanoes, hurricanes) that we experience today are directly related to the judgment of God in the Flood some 4,500 years ago.

Questions to Ponder

- In geology class, students are taught about a series of Ice Ages during the course of millions of years. How can an Ice Age (or Advance) be explained by the Flood model? Which is more compelling? How would you explain the model described in this chapter to your professor?
- Why would earthquakes and volcanoes be more frequent after the Flood than they are today? What evidence do we have that they were more powerful then?
- How could very warm oceans and very cold, bare continents following the Flood result in an Ice Age? Is there any evidence that this is the way it happened?
- As we view earth history in light of the aftermath of the Flood, how could the Grand Canyon have formed during the post-Flood period?

- It seems from the fossil record that new species appeared very rapidly in the centuries following the Flood. Evolution couldn't have accomplished it so quickly. Any idea what could?
- Explain to the skeptic how the animals coming off the ark could have migrated all over the world, settling in the climate that best suited their needs.
- Is there anything in this chapter that surprised you? Got your attention? Made you want to learn more? What questions did this chapter provoke in your thinking?
- What do we learn about God from what He has done in the post-Flood world?

A Verse to Remember

He removes mountains without their knowledge,
overturning them in His anger.
He shakes the earth from its place
so that its pillars tremble.
He commands the sun not to shine
and seals off the stars.

Job 9:5–7

CHAPTER 13

TO BABEL AND BEYOND

HOW can stories from the Book of Genesis about a tower and the confusion of languages intersect with twenty-first-century culture? Could they ever be relevant in a modern world? Yes, they are extremely relevant. The following campus incidents directly relate to the ancient histories of Genesis 10 and 11.

- In anthropology class: Students learn about Stone Age and Bronze Age civilizations. Other lessons include the familiar scenario of humans evolving from an apelike creature. All contradict the history of civilization found in the Book of Genesis.

- In the language department: Much ink and paper is spent discussing the origin of the bewildering assortment of languages in human history.

- In the history department: Students study Hitler and his concept of inferior/superior races. Hitler's application of one form of Social Darwinism (survival of the fittest races) led to the Holocaust—the destruction of six million Jewish people.

- Around the grounds: "Racial" issues dominate many extracurricular causes. Black, white, Asian, and Jewish people in various places and times are singled out for discrimination or attack. Yet the Bible is almost silent about the concept of race. An understanding of Genesis 10–11 tells us why.

- In the coffee house, dormitory, and apartment: The TV
  news and newspaper headlines excitedly report each new
  fossil "find," assuming man's evolutionary progression
  from the primates.

It seems that the ancient events in Babel *do* have relevance in
today's culture. Indeed, it may be strongly argued that Babel was a
pivotal event in earth history, even though it isn't likely to appear
as a chapter in a college history textbook.

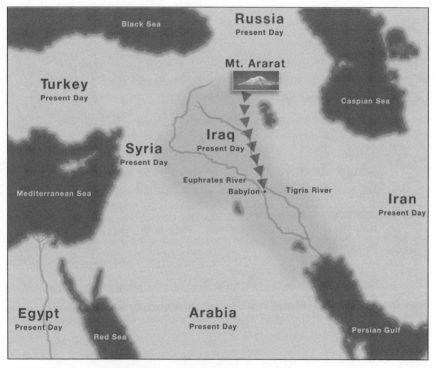

In Their Footsteps: From Ararat to Babel

*In Genesis 9:1, God told Noah's family after the Flood to "multiply and fill the
earth." Yet in the years between Ararat and the confrontation at Babel, this is as
far as most traveled. It seems the plains of Shinar (Babylon) were just too comfortable. The events of Genesis 10 would change all that.*

Erkel and Associates (Crozet, Va.)

Life after the Ark

When Noah and his family stepped off the ark, they entered a far different world than the one they lived in before the Flood. The antediluvian land was faulted, flooded, eroded, and buried under an average of one and one-half miles of sediment. All lakes and rivers, hills and mountains, and even the air and the soil were different. Plants and animals assembled into different communities and then began changing. Whatever animals and plants were sought before the Flood for medicine or food would be changing. Copper and iron would have to be searched for in new locations. Even with the highest cultural and technological ability, humans immediately after the Flood would have to live otherwise. Food would have to be gathered where it could be found, tools would have to be fashioned from crude materials, and shelter would have to be secured in different ways and places.

As conditions stabilized and resources could be found in their new locations, these hunting-gathering, stone-tool-based, cave-dwelling societies would change into agricultural, copper- and then iron-tool-based, city-dwelling societies. These changes, however, would occur in the course of decades to centuries—well within the course of a single human lifetime.

The first such transition must have led to the foundation of Babel's civilization.

The culture and technology developed before the Flood was probably preserved through the Flood in near-complete form. Noah had lived in the pre-Flood culture for six hundred years (Genesis 7:11), and his sons had lived in it for approximately one hundred years each (Genesis 5:32; 11:10). The ability to build a wooden ship the size of the ark would likely have required the use of whatever technology had been developed in pre-Flood times. We also know from Scripture that Noah (Genesis 9:28), Shem (Genesis 11:11), and probably the other sons of Noah lived for centuries after the Flood—well after the Babel incident, which involved the building of a city and a heaven-reaching tower that indicated a sophisticated culture that had survived the Flood.

When Did the Events of Babel Occur?

A review of the early biblical genealogies helps us make a fairly accurate guess concerning the time of the events at Babel. It is rather typical in the Bible to introduce a narrative with a genealogy. The Flood in Genesis 6–9, for example, is introduced by the genealogy in Genesis 5. Abraham's life story beginning in Genesis 12 is introduced by the genealogy in Genesis 11. In the same way, the Babel narrative of Genesis 11:1–9 is preceded by the genealogy of Genesis 10. Here, after the genealogy of each son of Noah (vv. 5, 20, and 31) and in the summary verse of the entire chapter (v. 32), we are told that the people of the post-Flood world eventually became "divided" according to language, family, and nation. The verses that follow (Genesis 11:1–9) describe specifically how it happened. It seems, then, that the purpose of the genealogy in Genesis 10 is to reveal the generations that led up to Babel.

Two generations of descendants are listed for Japheth, three generations for Ham, and five generations for Shem. In Shem's genealogy from Genesis 10 (v. 25), the son of Eber was named Peleg, "for during his days the earth was divided." In Shem's genealogy from Genesis 11, we see that Peleg was born 101 years after the Flood (by adding the figures in vv. 10, 12, 14 and 16) and died 340 years after the Flood (by adding the figures in vv. 18–19). We also learn from Genesis 10:25–29 that the division of languages apparently occurred after Peleg's thirteen nephews became heads of families. Since the average generation time in Genesis 11 is a bit more than thirty years, Peleg was probably more than eighty years old when Babel occurred. This means that Babel occurred sometime between the second half of the second century and the first half of the fourth century after the Flood.

What Happened at Babel and Why?

What is so bad about building a tower? Why did God intervene in the construction project? Of course, the story is a familiar one, but perhaps not so well understood. The understanding of Genesis 11:1 suggests that toward the end of the second century after the Flood, there was not only a single language (in the sense of a uniform set of words and linguistic rules) but also a single mental perspective or viewpoint. That all people were thinking similarly is certainly suggested by the fact that all the people banded together to build a single tower, probably under a single ruler, Nimrod (Genesis 10:10).

According to God's claim about the Babel event (Genesis 11:6), as long as all humans were unified, there was no limit to what they could do—including any *evil* they desired to do. His response was to divide the language. If that involved only the creation of a new set of words, however, it would have been relatively easy to translate from one language to another. Each word would simply have to be translated into the word of another person's language. But God desired to make communication among humans so impossible that they would scatter from one another over the entire earth (Genesis 11:9). Dividing not just the languages but also the perspectives (ways of thinking) would be the best way to accomplish this task.

At the end of the Babel event, it is likely that each family on earth had both a distinct language and a distinct perspective of the world. This is certainly consistent with the fact that, even today, learning a new language usually involves not only learning a new list of words but also a different way of thinking. Therefore, it is likely that the distinct cultures of the world arose as a direct result of the distinct languages and perspectives introduced to man at Babel.

In the Babel event, God created new languages and new ways of thinking. As was the case when He made things during Creation Week, God probably created these languages as already fully developed and these perspectives as fully mature. This would result in the instantaneous appearance of languages and the rapid origin of fully developed cultures. Different perspectives led people to create different expressions of culture. This is why different Babel families probably produced distinct forms of music, fine art, literature, and architecture.

From One to Many: Babel's Wide-Ranging Effects

- *Language.* There seems to be something on the order of a couple of hundred distinct language groups on earth—and no easy way to explain how these languages were derived from fewer earlier languages. This may point to the creation of languages at the tower of Babel. Among those languages, some of them developed written forms of communication. These written languages are so different from one another (from cuneiform to hieroglyphics to Chinese characters) that they also seem to confirm the sudden creation of language diversity at Babel. Furthermore, the age of the oldest evidences of those languages seems to decrease as we move away from the tower of Babel— apparently evidence of human dispersion away from that region.

- *Culture.* Cultures seem to show the same pattern. They appear on the scene rather fully developed and do not seem easily derivable from one another. Different language groups seem to have distinct musical forms and art perspectives not derivable from one another. The oldest evidences of human culture also seem to get younger away from the Middle East, which yields further evidence of human dispersion away from Babel. The extraordinary technologies evidenced in ancient cultures, such as the building of pyramids, sophisticated irrigation systems, huge statues and temples, seem to reflect the high culture that man was created with—a range of knowledge and skill that survived the Flood.

- *Worldviews and Ways of Thinking.* The Babel dispersion also provides a potential for comparative ethnology (study of human cultures), musicology, and study of comparative religions. For example, Western culture is dominated by the Indo-European language group. This branch developed a musical scale that is mathematically scaled off of actual sound waves in the physical world. It is also the culture that developed modern science—a mathematics-based study of the physical world. It developed the religion of naturalism—the belief that the physical world is all that exists. These similarities may be due to some sort of physical world perspective being given to the Indo-European ancestors at Babel.

- *Religion.* Noah and Shem (and probably the other sons of Noah) survived the Flood and lived at the time of Babel; they also believed God and knew the truth about Him. Noah, for example, had firsthand knowledge of more than one-third of earth history up to that point. He also lived for 42 years before the death of Adam's third son, Seth, who would have had firsthand knowledge of all but the first 130 years of the remaining two-thirds of earth history. Noah may then have had firsthand knowledge of one-third of earth history, secondhand knowledge of all but 130 years of the rest, and thirdhand knowledge of the first 130 years.

  It is likely, then, that everyone living at the time of Babel knew the true history of the world—about the one true God, the Creator of all things. And that same knowledge was carried away from Babel by all the peoples of the world, though understood in different languages and interpreted from different perspectives. According to Romans 1:21–32, even though all people once knew God, most have rejected Him and created their own religion. And these false religions were probably developed from the perspectives they were given at Babel. This may ultimately permit young-age creationists to explain why different cultures produced the particular kinds of music, art, architecture, and even religion that they developed.

- *Traditions.* The common knowledge possessed by all those who dispersed from Babel also explains similar traditions found in multiple cultures. Although each family group will likely distort the true stories over time—both in details and in chronology—similarities may be expected to persist. This would provide a good explanation for why more than 120 different cultures have Flood traditions and why so many of them have Creation and Fall traditions. Many cultures speak of a golden age of man—often before a world-destroying flood—when humans lived for a long time. The common knowledge at Babel would also explain the evidence in the oldest characters of the Chinese language that the earliest Chinese were monotheistic and believed the Creation and Fall accounts of Scripture.[1]

- *Races.* Only one family survived the Flood. It is likely, then, that even if there was more than one race before the Flood (and there is no hint in Scripture of this), only one race survived it. It is also likely that even by the time of Babel, there was still only one race. But the population may well have had a range of characteristics reflective of different races. And when the Babel event divided the human population into different languages and perspectives, it divided them according to their respective families.

  Because of the breakdown in communication, these families spread across the earth—each apparently going to a distinct place and separated from all other groups. Each family group became the start of a new people, which for many generations did not cross with any other family or people. Any physical differences that might have existed in the pre-Babel population were probably divided up among the different family groups—each one slightly different from the others.

  In each family group following the great dispersion, a phenomenon called *genetic drift* began to take over. Genetic drift occurs in small inbreeding populations, such as the families who were dispersed from Babel. It is really just a luck-of-the-draw problem. Take as an example the survival of surnames. Since women usually take on the surname of their spouse, surnames are generally passed down through the sons across the generations. Daughters eventually marry or die, thereby marking the end of the surname they carry. In large families with common names (such as Miller or Smith), it is unlikely that the family name will ever disappear. For this to happen, thousands of married couples would have to give birth to girls only. In small families, the chances are much greater that the family name could disappear because it would take just a few married couples bearing girls only.

In a similar way, genetic drift can take a given character trait that is not really more advantageous than any other and make it the only character trait in the population. Different skin colors, for example, do not cause a huge difference in human survival. Yet in small populations, genetic drift can eliminate the genetic information for all skin colors but one. In the generations following Babel, different families probably developed unique combinations of physical characteristics. Some of these combinations were distinct enough to define what we have come to call the human "races."

Once particular traits were fixed into a particular family group, those traits may well have influenced where that family chose to live. Dominantly tall and thin families would find cold environments very uncomfortable. Light-skinned families would probably tend to avoid the tropics because of the sensitivity to sunburn. Very dark-skinned families would tend to avoid high latitudes where there was not enough sunlight to penetrate the skin and allow Vitamin E production. This would explain why many of the human races ended up where they did. The recency and rapidity of these changes is certainly consistent with the very small changes that separate the different races. The differences are literally only skin deep.

The differences in skin color are primarily due to different amounts of melanin in the skin. Some of the skin color differences, as well as the differences in eye shape and lip fullness, are due to the distribution of subcutaneous (under the skin) fat. Even hair distribution is due to differences in the skin. There seem to be no measurable differences in any other characteristic.

Genetically, different skin colors can be generated in the course of a single generation. Pure-bred whites and blacks cannot produce anything other than whites and blacks, respectively. Genetic information has apparently been lost in those lineages, probably through genetic drift in the centuries following Babel. Most people know, however, that the marriage of a pure-bred black and a pure-bred white will generate children with a wide range of skin colors between white and black. In fact, it appears theoretically possible for a marriage of people with a particular set of DNA to generate children of just about every skin color in the next generation. The skin color of such a couple would be brown—reasonably enough the dominant skin color on the earth today. Another curious observation is that in descendants of each of the sons of Noah, there is a wide range of skin colors known—something that would be expected in the Babel model of human dispersion.

Cave Men?

What were these people like—those who were scattered by the hand of God from the tower of Babel? Arphaxad, the son of Shem, was born two years after the Flood and lived for 438 years (Genesis 11:10–13). He thus lived through not only the tower of Babel incident but most of the incredible changes of the post-Flood earth discussed in chapter 12. The period of time during which Arphaxad lived—and during which the generations following Babel lived—might be called the *Arphaxadian Epoch*.

Aside from things that occurred during the Flood, the Arphaxadian Epoch saw some of the most interesting geological and climatological events in earth history. During the same period some of the most interesting events in human history also occurred. Human longevity was dropping at a steady rate. Humans gathered in Babel and were then dispersed worldwide by a confusion of language. It was also during this period that most of the great races, religions, and cultures of mankind arose.

Once the family groups dispersed from Babel, each one would have found itself in "survival mode"—lacking shelter, agriculture, and metals for tools. In each situation, agriculture, metal working, and cities would have to be developed independently. The rate of culture development would vary considerably from location to location, some never moving out of the hunting-gathering mode at all. Most of the time, however, culture could develop through stages of stone tool development to copper and bronze tool development—and beyond—in the space of a single lifetime.

Then, like ripples from pebbles thrown into a pond, culture would move outward from cultural centers. At any given point in earth history after Babel, different cultures could be found in every different stage of cultural development—just as is the case today.

The most ancient cultural evidences of these activities are interpreted very differently in young-age creationism than any alternative model of earth history. A particular quality of stone tool, for example, is traditionally interpreted as indicating a particular period of earth history, as if that specific tool was made only at one time in earth history. In young-age creationism, however, the same potential for cultural evolution was possessed by numerous, closely related families at many different places across the earth. It is very likely that the same type of stone tool was developed independently by many different Babel families at many different locations on earth. At each location it was probably developed at a different time and was produced for a much briefer period than is thought in other theories.

The oldest cave paintings of the earth, then, are understood to be rather sophisticated paintings of a culturally capable people forced to survive in caves, forced for a time to eat what they could hunt and gather. The relatively low frequency of such cave sites, ancient burial sites, and even stone tools is better explained by rapid multiregional cultural evolution such as is suggested in young-age creation theory. The sophisticated clothing and artifacts found on "Ice Man"[2] and his inferred behavior is understandable in young-age creation theory, but it is rather difficult to explain in any other model.

A Case Study: Fossil Humans (Paleoanthropology)

Once more, let's put our principles into practice. The case in question: the long line of ape to human "hominid" forms whose artist rendition pictures regularly grace the cover of *National Geographic* and appear in every biology textbook and museum. No one who ever reads a newspaper could be immune from exposure to the claims of Paleoanthropology (the study of human and humanlike fossils). A trip to the chimpanzee exhibit at the local zoo is always good for a few well-placed comments on the evolution of man from apes.

The Bioevolutionary Story of Mankind

What evidence is presented for the ape to man progression of fossils that are so prominently displayed at museums and in text-books and magazines? Such fossils range (from older to younger) from generally scrappy (but occasionally good) specimens of African apes called australopithecines (including "Lucy"), to excellent and fairly common specimens of *Homo erectus* (including "Java Man" and "Peking Man"), to common specimens of Neanderthals and beautiful and common specimens of modern *Homo sapiens*.

In bioevolutionary theory, humans are thought to have evolved from some single-celled ancestor through a long series of forms before evolving from some apelike ancestor in the fairly recent past. In this theory, apes should not appear as fossils until well up into the fossil record and should appear before human fossils.

Furthermore, human traits should show up in a stepwise fashion through the fossil sequence. The fossil record seems to confirm these expectations, with apes not found as fossils until well up in the rock column, apes with humanlike characteristics (e.g., australopithecines, which may have walked upright) above the first ape fossils, and humanlike fossils (e.g., *Homo habilis* and *Homo erectus*) occurring even farther up. Furthermore, whereas the first tools were chipped rocks, subsequent tools were stone arrowheads. Evidence of hunting and gathering fruits and nuts occurs before evidence of agriculture, and evidence of cave-dwelling predates the building of cities. The fossil record shows evidence of the cultural evolution expected in evolutionary theory.

Does the Theory Conflict with Scripture?

Absolutely. The biblical account of the Creation of Adam and Eve cannot be reconciled to this evolutionary scenario.

Is There Another Way to Interpret the Data?

What are we to do when a theory contradicts biblical truth? We look at the data for an interpretation that is consistent with God's truth.

When Noah and his family left the ark, God spoke to him and gave a command He once gave to Adam and Eve: "Be fruitful and multiply and fill the earth" (Genesis 9:1). Although they were fruitful and multiplied, they were disobedient to the command to disperse. Perhaps the post-Flood catastrophic events frightened them and caused them to remain in a safe place. Perhaps they were merely comfortable staying together on the plain of Shinar in Babylon, where they built a city, a tower, and a government. But God forced them to disperse by dividing their language.

In the meantime, God had ordered creation in such a way that the animals and plants acted in accordance with His command and spread to the most distant places on the earth's surface. The humans would arrive later. This explains why animal fossils—including the fossils of apes—are found below the first evidences of humans. Evolutionary theories interpret this as evidence that humans evolved from a lower life form. But young-age creationists interpret this same evidence as another example of man's stubborn refusal to live the life God desires for him.

The humans who lived soon after the Flood lived under unusual circumstances. The changing plants and animals must have generated a changing and perhaps unreliable diet. This problem was made even worse by changes in medicinal plants as well as new diseases that arose through never-before-seen mutations. Remaining healthy was probably a great struggle for man just after the Flood. Humans in the Arphaxadian Epoch lived much longer than they do today. Noah lived more than nine centuries (Genesis 9:29). It is not known exactly how humans weathered such age. It is possible that with a longer life span, people matured more slowly. The ages of fathers at the birth of their sons average much higher before the Flood when life spans were longer. But ten generations after Noah, Abraham lived less than two centuries (Genesis 25:7).

The decrease in life span may have been partially caused by accelerated development. If so, this might explain why the first temporary teeth in children are coming in at earlier ages and why female menstrual cycles are starting at steadily earlier ages. And it may be the cause of much improper reconstruction of fossil humans.[3] The slower development of post-Flood people may have led to the development of a different stature and bone structure. These differences may account for some of the differences between living and fossil humans. Other differences may turn out to be due to different diet and climate.

Ultimately, fossils dubbed *Homo erectus* and *Homo sapiens* are almost certainly humans who lived in the first couple of centuries after the Babel dispersion. The brain size indicated by these fossils overlaps the range found in modern man. The bones (aside from the skull) can hardly be distinguished from modern humans. One of the oldest known *Homo erectus* skeletons is of what appears to be (at modern maturation rates) a sixteen-year-old boy who as an adult would stand more than six feet tall. The remaining fossils that have been interpreted by some as human or as ancestors of humans (the australopithecines) are interpreted by young-age creationists to be extinct apes that lived in the Arphaxadian Epoch with man. All these fossils have brain sizes well below that of modern humans and in or near the range of modern apes. Even the nonskull bones are relatively easily distinguished from modern man.

Young-age creationism interprets much of earth history very differently from alternate theories. We have dealt with many of them in this book. And, as we have often stated, much study and research remains to be done to see the truths of Scripture revealed in the evidence we hold in our hands or will uncover in the future. But young-age creationism does not have a totally divergent view of earth history. By about the time of King David, radiocarbon dates seem to correspond to biblical dates. Much of the conventional interpretation of archaeology from about 1000 B.C. and forward are interpreted very much the same as it is in other theories. We differ on many fronts, but we do share some points of agreement.

Summary: What We Learn about the Creator/Artist from What He Has Done

How exciting it is to see the hand of the Sovereign God throughout history! God's interest has always been for man to glorify Him in the entire creation. God's love for man has always been present, even when His holiness demands that He judge man for disobedience.

God "knows our frame," knows the sinfulness of mankind. He protected men from their own sinfulness by dividing them because in their unity the effects of evil they could accomplish would be ever so much stronger. Perhaps we should wonder today at what God thinks of our "one-world" mentality, with the instant communication afforded by the Internet and other technology.

In these short chapters we have witnessed three major judgments of a Holy God. The first was, of course, the Fall, which plunged mankind and the entire cosmos into a sea of corruption and death. But God the Merciful had provided a way of salvation, and He kept a remnant of people who would belong to Him.

The second judgment was the Flood, when again a righteous remnant was preserved through Noah and his family, and the world that was destroyed in the Flood was renewed and allowed to continue to bring glory to its Creator.

The third judgment was the judgment at Babel. Many people don't see this as a judgment, but actually something very significant and sad for mankind happened at Babel. After dispersing the people, God turned His focus to a particular people on whom to rest His love. From Shem's descendant Abram (later called Abraham) would come the Hebrew people. And from His chosen people would ultimately come One, God in the flesh, Who would offer redemption to all who would believe in Him. Through Abram/Abraham, all the families of the earth would be blessed, and that included the sons of Ham and Japheth, who had been dispersed and seemingly forgotten for a time. Even in the midst of judgment, our God remembers mercy.

What's Next?

As we have surveyed the broad subject of origins in this book, we have looked at the age of things, at God's creation of the universe, the earth, and living things. We have taken a lightning trip through earth history from Creation through the Fall, the Flood, and the dispersion of languages and nations at Babel. Our trip ends for our purposes at approximately the year 2000 B.C. There is of course another two thousand years of history to follow in the remaining chapters of Scripture, yet the origins—the beginnings—have here been reviewed.

In the last chapter to follow, we will seek to pull together the major concepts developed during this whirlwind tour of two thousand years of history. These principles have been often repeated during the book. Let's see how many you remember.

Consider the Concept

When God divided the languages and scattered families throughout the world, He was bringing another judgment on mankind that would single out one son of Noah and isolate two other sons from His special attention for centuries to come. God turned His face toward a particular son of Shem.

Questions to Ponder

- Explain the fossils australopithecines (e.g., Lucy), *Homo Erectus,* Neanderthals, and *Homo sapiens* to your anthropology professor (or your friend in youth group, or your pastor) in a God and Scripture-honoring way.
- Different languages—different cultures—different races—different nations. Explain their origin from a biblical perspective.
- If all of mankind descended from Noah and his three sons and spouses, how do we have such different skin colors?
- A naturalist speaks of stone-age and iron-age cultures. How would the creationist explain the different cultures?
- Is there anything in this chapter that surprised you? Got your attention? Made you want to learn more? What questions did this chapter provoke in your thinking?
- What do we learn about God from what He has done during this period of earth history?

A Verse to Remember

From one man He has made every nation of men to live all over the earth and has determined their appointed times and the boundaries of where they live.

Acts 17:26

Where will he be with the Lord ten years from now? Remembering certain vital principles will help him stay on track.

Heidi Howard, Erkel and Associates (Crozet, Va.)

CHAPTER 14
REMINDERS TO REMEMBER

THROUGHOUT this book, the story of a college student has been used to illustrate the value of the study of origins in dealing with the faith challenges that a person may encounter in the young adult years. Some of you will never be college students. Some of you have already completed your college education. Although the academic scene is a superb example of the confusing array of ideas and lifestyles that a young person encounters, it is by no means the only example. Challenges occur in virtually every season of life and in every setting where humans live their lives. Even as we grow older, we encounter ideas and experiences that cause us to question our faith.

The aging apostle Peter once wrote, "Therefore I will always remind you about these things, even though you know them and are established in the truth you have" (2 Peter 1:12). He went on in his epistle to tell once more the important things the believers needed to remember. His chief reminder was that they know and remember the Word of God as spoken through the prophets and the apostles (2 Peter 3:1–2).

We have communicated many things to you in this short book (although not on the level of infallible Scripture). We have sought to show you how the study of origins can impact your life in a fundamental way. Some ideas were no doubt new to you; others were things you "already knew." A danger we all face is that of succumbing to the attitude "Don't tell me that again; I already *know* that!"

Scripture affirms that we *need* to be reminded—often—of even the things we know.

This final chapter contains eight "reminders" of things you hopefully already know. These concepts express the heart of the authors of this book. Condensed into eight principles are the most vital truths to be gleaned from your reading. If you understand them, you truly "got" the message of this book.

1. Remember Why You Were Created

The Westminster Catechism answers the question "What is the chief aim of man?" with the answer "to glorify God and enjoy Him forever." Scripture abundantly affirms this principle. You have been uniquely created with the ability to know the Creator. You have seen in this book some of the ways you can know Him as you learn from what He has made. You have also seen that He created purposefully, with great beauty and detail. He has created you with particular natural and spiritual gifts, with a "style" all your own, and with unique interests. It is important to recognize the gifting and call that you have been given in order that you might glorify Him in the use of those gifts and abilities. If your gifting and interest is in the area of science, consider how you might honor Him through study of the natural world. For example, in this book are included areas of need for further origins research. If your intelligence is in language and literature, serve Him in the God-honoring use of the written and spoken word. If you have been gifted with skillful hands, then be the best plumber, builder, or artist you can be. Everything and everyone God created fulfills a purpose.

> Based on the gift they have received, everyone
> should use it to serve others, as good managers of the
> varied grace of God. If anyone speaks, [his speech
> should be] like the oracles of God; if anyone serves,
> [his service should be] from the strength God provides,
> so that in everything God may be glorified through
> Jesus Christ. To Him belong the glory and the power
> forever and ever. Amen. (1 Peter 4:10–11)

2. Remember to Keep Learning about the Artist from What He Has Made and What He Has Done

Learning does not end with a college degree or the close of professional training. The Hebrew sages "got it right" when they pronounced that learning is a lifetime privilege and responsibility. You are to be a student *forever!* God has provided ways for you to continue to grow in grace and knowledge both from studying His written Word and from studying His masterpiece, Creation. Even if you aren't a natural scientist by skill and training, there is much you can continue to learn and appreciate about the world God has made. Even if you don't consider yourself skilled in Bible study, you are told to read the Word and be diligent in study. This is the way we can fulfill the command to know the Lord and enjoy Him forever.

The LORD's works are great,
studied by all who delight in them.
(Psalm 111:2)

3. Remember That There Are Many Perspectives (Worldviews) from Which People Interpret the Facts and Events They Observe

In this the beginning of the twenty-first century, probably most people you encounter will have a worldview that differs from your own. When people with differing perspectives view the same facts (data), their explanation of those facts will also differ widely because of the worldview that influences them. For example, a person who doesn't believe in God could observe Jesus performing a miracle before his eyes and still deny that miracle. A person who does not believe in absolute truth will never have a solid ground on which to stand—all because of his framework for interpretation, his worldview.

It is extremely important for you to become a "worldview diagnostician." Whenever you read or hear explanations of data, you need to ask, "Where is this person coming from? Is this biblical? Is he a naturalist who denies any spiritual or biblical input? Is he a postmodern who denies any objective truth?" Interpretations can come from people who are extremely intelligent, and those explanations might be reasonable and even appealing, but they can be *wrong* because the perspectives behind the interpretations are wrong.

Let whoever is wise understand these things,
and whoever is insightful recognize them.
For the ways of the LORD are right,
and the righteous walk in them,
but the rebellious stumble in them.
(Hosea 14:9)

4. Remember What to Do When You Hear Interpretations of the World That Contradict the Clear Teaching of Scripture

The professor is brilliant! The reasoning behind the conclusions seems faultless. All the scholarly people are nodding their heads and clapping enthusiastically. But the professor has just trashed the Bible! If he is correct, much of what you have believed since you became a Christian is a lie.

So, do you go home and throw away your Bible and walk away from your profession of faith? Of course not. You remind yourself of principle 3 listed above. Ask, "Where is this person coming from? What is his worldview?" Then ask, "Is there *another* way of interpreting the same data? If one believes in a Creator God Who communicated absolute truth to His people, how should one think and proceed?" There always will be a way to explain God's world that is accurate and honoring to Him because, after all, it is *His* world, and He is the original and perfect Communicator. This book has introduced many interpretations of origins data that differ from the current conventional approach. These ideas are new and need further study, but they present plausible and exciting alternatives that hold to the truth of the Word of God and observations of His world.

Be careful that no one takes you captive through
philosophy and empty deceit based on human tradition, based on the elemental forces of the world, and
not based on Christ. (Colossians 2:8)

5. Remember to Stay Connected to the Body of Christ

Once you leave family and your home church, it is all too easy to fail to get involved with believers in your new location. Your new academic responsibilities or job demands are consuming, and it may become inconvenient to maintain the discipline of church attendance and study of Scripture.

You were not created to go it alone; you were created to be part of a body, in which each part supports and complements the other parts. The evil one loves to isolate and conquer. Become involved in a strong church where the gospel is preached in power. Find a Christian group, even one Christian brother or sister who will study with you, support you, and hold you accountable to walk in truth. Parachurch ministries, such as Intervarsity, Navigators, and Campus Crusade, are active at many colleges. Some universities have Christian Study Centers nearby for discipleship, fellowship, and growth. Look also for someone who can mentor you in the faith— a Christian faculty member or spiritually mature church member. Finally, stay in the Word—no subject you will ever study in school will be as important as the Word of God. Become engaged in a consistent Bible study with a committed group of believers, preferably an inductive Bible study that will teach you how to become a lifetime student of Scripture.

> And let us be concerned about one another in order
> to promote love and good works, not staying away
> from our meetings, as some habitually do, but encouraging each other, and all the more as you see the day
> drawing near. (Hebrews 10:24–25).

6. Remember What to Do When You Haven't Received Totally Satisfying Answers to Your Faith-Challenging Questions

God requires faith in order to please Him. Logic, reason, and knowledge play important roles, but faith must carry the day. If we could reason our way to God with proofs and evidence, then faith would not be necessary. Scripture teaches that we walk by faith and not sight (2 Corinthians 5:7).

So it seems that God will always keep us a little off balance when it comes to giving complete answers to everything we ever want to know. If we had those answers, we wouldn't need faith. He gives compelling evidence, exciting observations, but often stops short of total proof. That waits for the time when we will no longer "see indistinctly, as in a mirror" (1 Corinthians 13:12).

> Now without faith it is impossible to please God, for
> the one who draws near to Him must believe that He
> exists and rewards those who seek Him. (Hebrews 11:6)

7. Remember, You Are Responsible

> "Ah, Lord GOD! You Yourself made the heavens and
> earth by Your great power and with Your outstretched
> arm. Nothing is too difficult for You!." (Jeremiah 32:17)

Jeremiah, in his beautiful prayer, declares God's Sovereignty as shown by His work as Creator. Nothing is too difficult for Him. Therefore, He is in charge. Because He created you, you belong to Him. Because He loves you, He sent His Word, both written and living (through His Son), so that you might know how to live as He intends for you to live—for His glory. With that supreme truth comes responsibility. You are to obey, to "follow the rules" He has given you, to walk the way He teaches you to walk. He gives you the rules because He as your Creator loves you and knows how you can be all you were created to be. May He grant you grace as you continue on the path.

> Our Lord and God,
> You are worthy to receive
> glory and honor and power,
> because You have created all things,
> and because of Your will
> they exist and were created.
> (Revelation 4:11)

8. Remember the Rest of the Story: Jesus

This final principle has eternal value and needs to be remembered above all others. Even before God created the world and mankind plunged the world into sin, redemption had been planned and provided through the One Who would come to die and be raised again (Revelation 13:8). *Remember Jesus.* None of it makes any sense without Him. Remember also that there will be another judgment to come, the final judgment. There is clearly only one way to escape the final judgment, and that is through believing in the Lamb of God who has provided that way of escape.

Most who read this book are "churched" people. You have most likely heard the gospel and participated in the life of a church. But have you *really* heard and responded? Have you worked through the doubts and uncertainties? Could you perhaps be playing the part of a dutiful family member, but have not yet examined your own heart to see if you have made the message your own? Be certain of His calling and choosing you—the stakes are too great both in this world and the next.

Therefore, brothers, make every effort to confirm
your calling and election, because if you do these
things you will never stumble. (2 Peter 1:10)

NOTES

Chapter 1. A Young Person Goes to College

1. Quoted in talk by Jeff Myers, May 2001. Myers reported data from Alexander Astin's Freshman Survey conducted every year with freshmen at colleges across America (this data reported in late '80s).

Chapter 2. God's Word and God's World

1. For a detailed discussion of this topic, see Henry M. Morris, *Men of Science, Men of God* (Green Forest, Ark.: Master Books, 1988).

Chapter 3. How Old Is *Old?*

1. Gary Phillips and David Fouts, "Genesis 1–11 as Historical Narrative" at www.harborlighthouse.com

2. Andrew A. Snelling, "Geochemical Processes in the Mantle and Crust," in Vardiman et al., *Radioisotopes and the Age of the Earth* (Santee, Calif.: Institute for Creation Research, 2000), 126–31.

3. The National Geochronological Database (USGS Digital Data Series DDS-14, 1995) contains thousands of examples of rocks dated with multiple methods. A careful examination of these records shows that the methods rarely yield the same age.

4. Larry Vardiman, "Age of the Earth's Atmosphere Estimated by Its Helium Content," *Proceedings of the First International Conference on Creationism* (Pittsburgh: Creation Science Fellowship, 1986), 2:187–95.

5. E. F. Chaffin, "Theoretical Mechanisms of Accelerated Radioactive Decay," 305–31, and D. Russell Humphreys, "Accelerated Nuclear Decay: A Viable Hypothesis," 333–79, in Vardiman et al., *Radioisotopes and the Age of the Earth* (Santee, Calif.: Institute for Creation Research, 2000).

6. Larry Vardiman, "Ice Cores and the Age of the Earth," *Impact* 226 i-iv, (Santee, Calif.: Institute for Creation Research, 1992).

7. For further information, consult the following articles: D. Russell Humphries, "Reversals of the Earth's Magnetic Field during the Genesis Flood" in Walsh, *Proceedings of the First International Conference on Creationism* (Pittsburgh: Creation Science Fellowship, 1987), 113–26; D. W. Branette and John R. Baumgardner, "Patterns of Ocean Circulation over the Continents during Noah's Flood," Walsh, *Proceedings of the Second International Conference on Creationism* (Pittsburgh: Creation Science Fellowship, 1994), 77–86; and Larry Vardiman, "Numerical Simulation of Precipitation Induced by Hot Mid-Ocean

Ridges," 595–618, in Walsh, *Proceedings of the Third International Conference on Creationism* (Pittsburgh: Creation Science Fellowship, 1998), 595–618.

Chapter 4. God Created the Heavens

1. For a list of Anthropic Principle claims and references, see Wise and Cooper, "A Compelling Creation," *Proceedings of the Fourth International Conference on Creationism* (Pittsburgh: Creation Science Fellowship, 1998). A few of the many sources written by unbelievers include R. Breuer, *The Anthropic Principle: Man as the Focal Point of Nature* (Boston: Birkhauser, 1991)—an English translation by H. Newman and M. Lowey of a book published in German in 1981; J. D. Barrow and F. J. Tipler, *The Anthropic Cosmological Principle* (New York: Oxford University Press, 1986); J. Leslie, *Universes* (New York: Routledge, 1989); and M. A. Corey, *God and the New Cosmology: The Anthropic Design Argument* (Lanham, Md.: Rowman and Littlefield, 1993). Each of the Anthropic Principle evidences discussed in our text can be found (with a large number of others) in these secular sources.

2. Breuer, *The Anthropic Principle,* 233–37; Leslie, *Universes,* 59.

3. D. Faulkner, "The Current State of Creation Astronomy," *Proceedings of the Fourth International Conference on Creationism* (Pittsburgh: Creation Science Fellowship, 1998), 201–16.

Chapter 5. God Created the Earth

1. For further details see Kurt P. Wise, *Faith, Form, and Time* (Nashville: Broadman and Holman, 2002).

Chapter 6. God Created Living Things

1. Quote from Eugenia Scott in *Icons of Evolution,* DVD (Illustra Media, 2001).

2. Michael Behe, *Darwin's Black Box: The Biochemical Challenge to Evolution* (New York: The Free Press, 1996).

3. For an excellent and detailed presentation of baraminology, see Todd C. Wood and Megan J. Murray, *Understanding the Patterns of Life* (Nashville: Broadman and Holman, 2003).

4. Kurt P. Wise, *Faith, Form, and Time* (Nashville: Broadman and Holman, 2002), 126.

5. Ibid., 131.

Chapter 7. God Created Mankind

1. For further detail see Kurt P. Wise, *Faith, Form, and Time* (Nashville: Broadman and Holman, 2002), 140–48.

Chapter 8. Life before the Fall

1. For further detail see Kurt P. Wise, *Faith, Form, and Time* (Nashville: Broadman and Holman, 2002), 149–56.

Chapter 9. The Fall

1. For further information see Kurt P. Wise, *Faith, Form, and Time* (Nashville: Broadman and Holman, 2002), 157–69.

Chapter 10. Life before the Flood
1. J. Scheven, "Floating Forests on Firm Ground," *Journal of the Biblical Creation Society,* 3(9):36–43, 1981. Kurt P. Wise, "The Pre-Flood Floating Forest: A Study in Paleontological Pattern Recognition," *Proceedings of the Fifth International Conference on Creationism* (Pittsburgh: Creation Science Fellowship, 2003).

Chapter 11. The Flood
1. John C. Whitcomb Jr., and Henry M. Morris, *The Genesis Flood: The Biblical Record and Its Scientific Implications* (Phillipsburgh, N.J.: Presbyterian and Reformed, 1961), 1–35.

2. Steven Austin et al., "Catastrophic Plate Tectonics: A Global Flood Model of Earth History," *Proceedings of the Third International Conference on Creationism* (Pittsburgh: Creation Science Fellowship, 1994), 609–21.

3. John Baumgardner, "Computer Modeling" and "Runaway Subduction as the Driving Mechanism for the Genesis Flood," *Proceedings of the Third International Conference on Creationism* (Pittsburgh: Creation Science Fellowship, 1994).

4. D. Russell Humphreys, "Reversal of the Earth's Magnetic Field," *Proceedings of the First International Conference on Creationism* (Pittsburgh: Creation Science Fellowship, 1986), 2:113–26; and D. Russell Humphreys, "Physical Mechanism for Reversal of the Earth's Magnetic Field," *Proceedings of the Second International Conference on Creationism* (Pittsburgh: Creation Science Fellowship, 1990), 2:129–42.

5. Arthur Chadwick, "Lithologic Paleogeographic and Paleocurrent Maps of the World" in http://chadwicka.swac.edu

6. Kurt P. Wise, "The Fossil Record: The Ultimate Test Case for Young-Earth Creationism," *Opus: A Journal for Interdisciplinary Studies* 1991–92: 17–29.

7. Steven A. Austin, "Geologic Structure of the Grand Canyon," *Grand Canyon: Monument to Catastrophe* (Santee, Calif.: Institute for Creation Research, 1994), 9–19.

8. Ibid., 21–56.

9. D. Faulkner, "A Biblically-Based Cratering Theory," *CENTJ* 13(1):100–104.

Chapter 12. The Post-Flood World
1. Larry Vardiman, "A Conceptional Transitional Model," *Proceedings of the Third International Conference on Creationism* (Pittsburgh: Creation Science Fellowship, 1994), 3:569–79 and "Numerical Simulation of Precipitation," *Proceedings of the Fourth International Conference on Creationism* (Pittsburgh: Creation Science Fellowship, 1998), 4:607–18.

2. Steven Austin, "How Was the Grand Canyon Eroded?" *The Grand Canyon: Monument to Catastrophe* (Santee, Calif.: Institute for Creation Research, 1994).

3. This transition is documented by the change in pollen as one passes up through Tertiary sediments (see Thure E. Cerling and James R. Ehleringer, "Welcome to the C4 World," in Robert A. Gastaldo and William A. DiMichele [conveners], *Phanerozoic Terrestrial Ecosystems* [The Paleontological Society, USA, 2000], 273–86.)

4. J. F. McCauley et al., "Subsurface Valley and Geoarchaeology of the Eastern Sahara Revealed by Shuttle Radar," *Science* 218 (1982): 1004–20; and H.

J. Pachur and S. Kropelin, "Wadi Howar: Paleoclimate Evidence from an Extinct River System in the Southeastern Sahara," *Science* 237 (1987): 298–300.

5. R. M. Schoch and J. A. West, "Further Evidence Supporting a Pre-2500 B.C. Date for the Great Sphinx of Giza, Egypt," *GSA Abstracts with Programs* 32(7) (2000): A276.

6. Todd C. Wood, "Perspectives on AGEing, A Young-Earth Creation Diversification Model," in *Proceedings of the Fifth International Conference on Creationism* (Pittsburgh: Creation Science Fellowship, 2003): 479-489.

7. Kurt P. Wise and M. Croxton, "Rafting: A Post-Flood Biogeographic Dispersal Mechanism," in *Proceedings of the Fifth International Conference on Creationism* (Pittsburgh: Creation Science Fellowship, 2001), 465-78.

Chapter 13. To Babel and Beyond

1. Jerry Bergman, "Creation and Creation Myths," *Creation Research Society Quarterly* 30(4):205–12.

2. Greg Beasley, "A Possible Creationist Perspective on the Tyrolean (Oetztaler) Ice Man," *Creation Ex Nihilo Technical Journal* 8(2) (1994): 179–91.

3. John W. Cuozzo, "Neanderthal Children's Fossils: Reconstruction and Interpretation Distorted by Assumptions," *Creation Ex Nihilo Technical Journal* 8(2) (1994): 166–78.

DIGGING DEEPER: SUGGESTIONS FOR FURTHER STUDY

Arthur, Kay, Sheila Richardson, and Kurt P. Wise. *Genesis Precept upon Precept Part 1: Creation.* Chattanooga: Precept Ministries International, 1998.
  An inductive Bible study on Genesis chapters 1–2 that firmly establishes one in the Word of God. Also available: A series of video lectures by Dr. Kurt Wise on each lesson.

Arthur, Kay, Sheila Richardson, and Kurt P. Wise. *Genesis Precept upon Precept Part 2: The Fall, the Flood, the Nations.* Chattanooga: Precept Ministries International, 1999.
  An inductive Bible study on Genesis chapters 3–11 that firmly establishes one in the Word of God. Also available: A series of video lectures by Dr. Kurt Wise on each lesson.

Austin, Steven, ed. *Grand Canyon: Monument to Catastrophe.* Santee, Calif.: Institute for Creation Research, 1994.
  A colorful book that presents a positive model of origins in geology, biology, and anthropology through study of the Grand Canyon.

Behe, Michael J. *Darwin's Black Box.* New York: The Free Press, 1996.
  This is an antievolution book that focuses on Intelligent Design and irreducible complexity, written by a biochemist.

Brand, Leonard. *Faith, Reason, and Earth History.* Berrien Springs, Mich.: Andrews University Press, 1997.
  An excellent presentation of the paradigm of earth and biological origins by intelligent design. Scholarly. Detailed.

Colson, Charles and Nancy Pearcey. *How Now Shall We Live?*
Wheaton, Ill.: Tyndale House Publishers, 1999.
     How to build a biblical worldview in every area of life.
Denton, Michael. *Evolution: A Theory in Crisis.* Bethesda, Md.:
Adler and Adler, 1986.
     *Anti-Darwinism. Written by a non-Christian molecular
     biologist. Technical information suitable for those with
     some scientific background.*
Johnson, Phillip E. *Darwin on Trial.* Washington, D.C.: Regnery
Gateway, 1991.
     *Anti-Darwinism. Written from the perspective of logic
     and philosophy. No biblical content. A book foundational to
     the Intelligent Design movement.*
Johnson, Phillip E. *Defeating Darwinism by Opening Minds.* Downers
Grove: InterVarsity Press, 1997.
     *Gives strategies to combat the dogma found on campus
     (and elsewhere).*
Morris, Henry M. *The Biblical Basis for Modern Science.* Green
Forest, Ariz.: Master Books, 2002.
     *A revision of a classic. Biblical foundation for all sci-
     ences.*
Wells, Jonathan. *Icons of Evolution.* New York: Regnery, 2000.
     *Antievolution material that focuses on refuting particu-
     lar, well-used arguments found in most textbooks.*
Wise, Kurt P. *Faith, Form, and Time: What the Bible Teaches and
Science Confirms about Creation and the Age of the Universe.*
Nashville: Broadman and Holman Publishers, 2002.
     *This is a more detailed version of the book you have just
     read. Establishes a biblical and positive model of origins.*
Wood, Todd Charles and Megan J. Murray. *Understanding the
Patterns of Life.* Nashville: Broadman and Holman Publishers,
2003.
     *Establishing the biological model of origins through the
     study of baraminology.*

Also Available

The TruthQuest™ Inductive Student Bible (NLT)
    Black bonded leather with slide tab 1-55819-843-1
    Blue bonded leather with slide tab 1-55819-849-0
    Paperback with Expedition Bible Cover 1-55819-928-4
    Hardcover 1-55819-855-5
    Paperback 1-55819-848-2
    Expedition Bible Cover only 1-55819-929-2

***The TruthQuest™ Share Jesus without Fear
New Testament*** (HCSB) 1-58640-013-4

The TruthQuest™ Prayer Journal 0-8054-3777-0

The TruthQuest™ Devotional Journal 0-8054-3800-9

TruthQuest™ Books _____

**Survival Guide:
The Quest Begins!**
by Steve Keels with Dan Vorm
(0-8054-2485-7)

Survival Guide Spanish Edition
**En Busca de la Verdad—
Plan de Accion**
(0-8054-3045-8)
Coming May 1, 2004

**You Are Not Your Own:
Living Loud for God**
by Jason Perry of Plus One with
Steve Keels (0-8054-2591-8)

**Living Loud:
Defending Your Faith**
by Norman Geisler and Joseph
Holden (0-8054-2482-2)

**Getting Deep: Understand
What You Believe about
God and Why**
by Gregg R. Allison
(0-8054-2554-3)

**Am I the One?: Clues to
Becoming and Finding a
Person Worth Marrying**
by James R. Lucas
(0-8054-2573-X)

**Vision Moments: Creating
Lasting Truths in the Lives
of Your Students**
by Bo Boshers and Keith Cote
(0-8054-2725-2)

Commentaries

Coming July 1, 2004
**Getting Deep
in the Book of . . .**
    Luke: Up Close with Jesus
    (0-8054-2852-6)
    **Romans: A Life and Death
    Experience** (0-8054-2857-7)
    James: Christian to the Core
    (0-8054-2853-4)
    Revelation: Never Say Die
    (0-8054-2854-2)
by Steve Keels
and Lawrence Kimbrough

Available at Your Local Book Retailer

BROADMAN
&HOLMAN
PUBLISHERS

www.broadmanholman.com/truthquest